My Sixty Years on the Plains

My Sixty Years on the Plains

Trapping, Trading, and Indian Fighting

By

William Thomas Hamilton

Enhanced Media
2017

My Sixty Years on the Plains - Trapping, Trading, and Indian Fighting by William Thomas Hamilton. First published in 1905.

This edition published 2017 by Enhanced Media. All rights reserved.

Enhanced Media Publishing
Los Angeles, CA.

First Printing: 2017.

ISBN-13: 978-1542771177

ISBN-10: 154277117X

Contents

CHAPTER I

On the river Till, in Cheviot Hills, Scotland, in the year 1825, twenty-five men formed a company for the purpose of emigrating. These men built themselves a bark, and when ready to sail held a council to determine whether their destination would be India or America. A vote was taken, which resulted in a tie, thus forcing the captain to cast his ballot. He voted for America, and by so doing destined me to fight Indians instead of hunting Bengal tigers in India. My father was one of the company, and his brother was the captain. I was just two years and ten months of age when we landed at New Orleans. My father had means and we travelled all over the States, finally settling in St. Louis eighteen months later. Here I remained until I was twenty years of age, receiving five years of schooling.

In the meantime chills and fevers were undermining my constitution, and the doctor ordered a change of climate. My father made arrangements with a party of hunters and trappers, who were in St. Louis at the time, to allow me to accompany them on their next trip, which would last a year.

The party consisted of eight men, all free trappers, with Bill Williams and Perkins as leaders. These two men had had fifteen years' experience on the plains amongst Indians, and had a wide reputation for fearless courage and daring exploits.

A good trading outfit was purchased, one third of which my father paid for, giving me a corresponding interest in the trip.

We started in the spring of 1842 with wagons and pack animals, making for Independence, Mo., which was the headquarters for all mountaineers in those days. At Independence we sold our wagons and rigged up a complete pack outfit, as our route would take us where it would be difficult for wagons to travel.

I was still wearing my city clothes, and mountain men present asked Williams what he was going to do with that city lad in the mountains. This remark cut me deeply, and I hurried to the frontier store and traded all my fine clothes, shirts, and dickeys, which were worn in those days, for two suits of the finest buckskin, such as these merchants always kept on hand to fleece greenhorns like myself, making five hundred per cent, profit in the trade. Next morning I appeared dressed a la prairie, and the old trappers noticed the change and said, "Williams, that boy of yours will make a mountaineer if he catches on at this rate."

We all went to work getting our pack outfit ready, which was accomplished before night. Next morning, the 15th of March, 1842, we started, bidding adieu to the remaining mountain men, who were all making preparations to start on their different routes for trapping and trading. The trappers and traders of that day were brave and reckless men, who never gave a second thought to the danger in their calling.

We made good time and reached Salt Creek on March 20th. Camp had just been made when we saw in the distance a small herd of buffalo coming directly towards us. Williams gave orders to corral all stock. No second order was needed with these mountain men, who acted in unison like a flash when occasion called for action. The stock was barely secured when the buffalo passed in close vicinity of camp, followed by thirty painted Kiowa warriors. A wild and savage-looking outfit they were. I had seen many Indians in St. Louis at different times, but none so wild and savage as these were. It was at this time that I received my first lesson in how to deal with wild Indians, or, more properly speaking, how to control their overt acts.

Our packs were placed in a triangle, answering in case of need to a good breastwork. Each man was armed with a rifle, two pistols, a tomahawk, and a large knife, commonly called "tooth-picker." Besides this, two of our men had bows and arrows, and were experts with them.

The Indians came up and examined our outfit and demanded pay for passing through their country. Williams gave them to understand that they could not go through the outfit, nor would they receive pay for passing through the country, informing them that this was Pawnee country. The Kiowas at that time were semi hostile, robbing and killing when it could be done with impunity.

I stood by Williams during the parley, much interested in the conversation, which was entirely by signs. The rest of the men were in what we called our fort, with stern and savage looks on their faces.

Williams was well up in Indian ways and treatment in any and every emergency, and finally gave the leader, or chief, as he called himself, some tobacco. They departed, looking daggers at us.

Williams informed me that there was no chief in the outfit, and that it was only a small thieving party led by a young brave, who had two feathers stuck in his scalp-lock.

We kept close watch during the night, expecting that the Indians would attempt to steal some of our stock or attack camp. Old experienced mountain men leave nothing to chance. Many outfits, within my knowledge, have come to grief through placing confidence in the red man, who always covets the belongings of the paleface.

Nothing disturbed us during the night, and in the morning we started down Salt Creek to the Platte River, where Williams expected to find Cheyennes, hoping to trade them out of some furs. We travelled up the Platte River to Cherry Creek, seeing plenty of fresh Indian signs, but no Indians.

The camp was kept well supplied with buffalo and antelope steak and ribs. The ribs are specially fine, and are highly appreciated by every one, whether mountaineer or dweller in civilization.

We camped on the North Platte River about two miles below where Cherry Creek empties; and about sundown three young Indians, who had been scouting for hostiles, rode into camp. They were Cheyennes, and the very ones that Williams was looking for, as they were generally well supplied with all kinds of furs. The Indians told us that their village was a short distance up the creek. Williams gave them tobacco for their chief, old White Antelope, and told them that we would visit the village on the following day. He then invited them to supper for the purpose of finding out what the tribe was most in need of, which is quite a trick in trading with Indians, though I believe the same rule works with white men. At all events, I never knew it to fail to bring a good trade.

We packed up early the following morning, but not before a few Indians had paid us a visit. They were elated at our coming, for they were acquainted with Williams and Perkins, with whom they had often traded, and were on what is called friendly terms. Perkins was the equal of Williams in knowledge of Indian science and, like him, was brave, cool, and ready in extreme danger.

We arrived at the village about eleven o'clock, preceded by our leaders, who wished to select the most advantageous camp, as it was our intention to remain several days.

We unpacked and put up a wall tent, which we used for a store. Our stock was put in the chief's care; and we supplied the women with all the necessaries for a feast. This is always customary if you wish to stand well, and must be given offhand and with generous impulse. Indians are close observers, and if they see that you give with a niggardly hand, they will say, "These white men love their goods, and will give us poor trade. Let's trade nothing but our poorest furs." Such an unfavorable condition must be avoided at any cost, as any trader will agree who has had experience among Indians.

Williams and Perkins had but a limited knowledge of sign-language, but sufficient to do the trading. All these signs I learned easily, much to their astonishment. They both claimed that they would never become experts, but that if I kept on in the way I had started I would soon be the most perfect of any white man on the plains. It came to me without any effort and certainly surprised me. The other men had been observing my aptness and were astonished. They were indifferent sign-talkers, but good in everything else that goes to make a thorough mountaineer. It has always appeared strange to me that so many intelligent men, who had been for so many years among Indians, trading and otherwise, were so deficient in knowledge of sign-language. Some assert that facility in the language is due to linguistic talent; but be that as it may, as I said before, the art was acquired by me without any effort.

All the principal chiefs assembled in White Antelope's lodge, where the customary smoke was indulged in, during which we were questioned as to what our outfit consisted of. Then came the feast, which included buffalo tongue, the choicest of meats, coffee, hardtack, and molasses. This last article is a favorite with all Indians.

In the meantime, Noble, Docket, and myself spread on blankets the various goods which Williams had selected for this trade,—powder, half-ounce balls, flints, beads, paint, blue and scarlet cloths, blankets, calico, and knives.

A certain rule must be complied with in trading with Indians, which is that you must not pay one Indian—man or woman—one iota more for a robe or fur of the same quality than you pay another. If you do, you ruin your trade and create antagonistic feelings throughout the village.

The Indians stood in need of all the articles named, and by sundown our tent was full of furs of the finest quality. We then adjourned for supper, which was prepared by the women.

After supper I accompanied the chief's son, Swift Runner, through the village. He was about my own age and took a great liking to me, taking considerable pains in teaching me signs. He introduced me to all the leading men in the village, telling them that I was his friend. I took special notice of a tall young boy with a particularly large nose, a magnificent specimen of a coming warrior. He was known as Big Nose; but I firmly believe he was the famous Roman Nose, who was killed by General Forsyth on the Republican River in 1868.

Swift Runner told me that a large hunting party was going to start the next morning after buffalo; and that if I would like to go he would furnish me with a good buffalo horse. I asked permission of Williams, and he consented, saying, "All right, boy; you can take my horse; he is one of the best buffalo horses on the plains." I thanked him, saying that Swift Runner had promised me one of his. The evening passed very pleasantly for me, as the young folks entertained me to the best of their ability.

I was considered fairly good-looking, with smooth face, agile and quick in movements. I was the youngest child and my parents had allowed me every indulgence. They owned a farm just outside of St. Louis, and I always claimed that I was a country raised boy. Foxes, deer, and coons were in abundance, and it followed that every boy would own a pony, providing, of course, that the parents could afford it. At all events, I possessed one of the best mustangs in Missouri—a little devil, which would kick at everything and everybody who approached him except myself. My brothers would say that we were a well-matched pair, both little devils. At home we indulged in all kinds of athletic exercises, such as dumb-bells, boxing, trapeze, and single-stick; and then we had constant practice with rifle and pistol, in all of which I became very proficient. I believe that all boys should be taught in the same way. It is productive of longevity, all things being physically equal. I am at this writing past eighty-one, straight as an arrow, supple and quick. I have never had use for glasses. Almost every day some one asks me to what I attribute my suppleness and eyesight, and I answer that "common-sense philosophy conforms to the teachings of hygiene."

CHAPTER II

The next morning, before daylight, fifty hunters and about twenty squaws with pack animals were assembled, ready to start on the buffalo hunt. We travelled about ten miles, when the scouts discovered a herd and reported their location to the hunting chief. He was thoroughly acquainted with the topography of the country and led us on a long detour, so as to get on the leeward side of the herd. As soon as we reached there, the Indians stripped to breech-clout and advanced, leading their running horses.

The chief now divided the hunters in two divisions, in order to get what buffalo were wanted in the smallest possible area. It is necessary to approach as close as possible before raising the herd, for when raised they travel fast and no laggard of a horse can overtake them.

Generally each division has a leader, who gives the order to go. We rode to within a quarter of a mile of the herd before the word was given.

Here would have been a grand scene for an artist to put on canvas—this wild array of naked Indians, sending forth yell after yell and riding like demons in their eagerness to bring down the first buffalo. For this is quite a feat and is commented upon by the whole village.

Swift Runner and his cousin had the fastest horses in our division and brought down the first buffalo, much to the chagrin of many a young brave, who coveted that honor that they might receive smiles from their lady loves.

My pony was close, on the heels of the leaders, and Swift Runner pointed out a fat cow for me. In a few jumps I was alongside and fired, greenhorn like, at the cow's kidneys. As luck would have it, however, I broke her back and she dropped. Swift Runner gave a yell of delight at my success. I should have put the shot just behind the shoulder.

There was yelling and shooting in every direction; and many riderless ponies were mixed in with the buffalo, with Indians after them, reckless if they in turn were dismounted as their friends had been, by the ponies stepping into prairie-dog or badger holes. Many an Indian has come to grief by having an arm or leg broken in this way. Ponies are sure-footed, but in a run such as this one, where over a thousand buffalo are tearing at full speed over the prairie, a dust is created which makes it impossible for the ponies to see the holes, hence the mishaps, which are very common.

All the meat required lay in an area of three quarters of a mile. I had brought down four and received great praise from the Indians. I could have done much better, but, boy-like, I wanted to see the Indians shoot their arrows, which many of them used. One arrow was sufficient to bring the buffalo to its knees. They shot behind the shoulder, sending the arrow deep enough to strike the lungs. One shot there is enough for any animal in the United States.

Now came the butchering, which was completed in two hours, and each pony was packed with three hundred pounds of the choicest of meat.

Several Indians who had been thrown, limped somewhat, but none were seriously hurt.

We arrived at the village about sundown and found the whole tribe lined up to greet us and to ascertain how successful we had been.

A feast had been prepared and was awaiting our coming; and as for myself, I was "wolfish," —which is a mountain man's expression for hungry,—for I had tasted no food since five o'clock in the morning.

After supper incidents of the hunt were gone over, and listened to with interest by all. Our party congratulated me warmly on my success, and it was commented on also by the Indians, which pleased the boys immensely. If a white man fails to acquit himself creditably it invariably casts a reflection on all whites.

The Cheyennes were and are today a proud and brave people. Their domestic habits were commendable and could be followed to advantage by many white families. To violate the marriage vow meant death or mutilation. This is a rule which does not apply to all tribes. Meat is their principal food, although berries of different kinds are collected in season, as well as various roots. The kettle is on the tripod night and day. They use salt when they can get it, and are very fond of molasses, sugar, coffee, and flour. They are hospitable to those whom they respect, and the reverse to those for whom they have contempt.

Most tribes of plains Indians dry their meat by cutting it in thin flakes and spreading it on racks and poles in the sun; although in damp or wet weather it is put inside of lodges, where it will dry, but not so well as in the sun. Mountain men follow the same practice and use the meat when game is scarce, and this often occurs.

Pemmican is manufactured in the following manner. The choicest cuts of meat are selected and cut into flakes and dried. Then all the marrow is collected and the best of the tallow, which are dissolved together over a slow fire to prevent burning. Many tribes use berries in their pemmican. Mountaineers always do unless they have sugar. The meat is now pulverized to the consistency of mincemeat; the squaws generally doing this on a flat rock, using a pestle, many specimens of which may be seen on exhibition in museums. A layer of meat is spread, about two inches thick, the squaws using a wooden dipper, a buffalo horn, or a claw for this work. On this meat is spread a certain amount of the ingredients made from the marrow and tallow, the proportion depending on the taste. This same process is repeated until the required amount is secured. One pound of pemmican is equal to five pounds of meat.

Buffalo tongues are split the long way and dried for future use, and thus prepared are a delicacy fit for a prince.

Another important article of food, the equal of which is not to be had except from the buffalo, is "depuyer" (dipouille). It is a fat substance that lies along the backbone, next to the hide, running from the shoulder-blade to the last rib, and is about as thick as one's hand or finger. It is from seven to eleven inches broad, tapering to a feather edge on the lower side. It will weigh from five to eleven pounds, according to the size and condition of the animal. This substance is taken off and dipped in hot grease for half a minute, then is hung up inside of a lodge to dry and smoke for twelve hours. It will keep indefinitely, and is used as a substitute for bread, but is superior to any bread that was ever made. It is eaten with the lean and dried meat, and is tender and sweet and very nourishing, for it seems to satisfy the appetite. When going on the war-path the Indians would take some dried meat and some depuyer to live on, and nothing else, not even if they were to be gone for months.

I have been asked many times regarding depuyer by different ones who have been astonished when told of its merits as a substitute for other food, and surprised that it was so little known except by mountain men and Indians. Trappers would pay a dollar a pound for it, and I do not believe that bread would bring that price unless one were starving. As I have said, it is a substitute for bread; and when you are invited to an Indian lodge your host will present you with depuyer just as you would present bread to a guest. You may be sure should they fail to present you with depuyer that you are an unwelcome guest.

Williams concluded to move the next day, so he traded for a few ponies, sufficient to pack the furs for which we had traded.

When we were ready to start, the leading chiefs assembled to say good-bye ("how"), and the women presented me with a half-dozen pairs of beautifully embroidered moccasins. This tribe excels all others in bead-work as well as in garnishing and painting robes. One must bear in mind, however, that the Cheyennes of 1842 must not be classed with the Cheyennes of today.

When I parted from my young Indian friend Swift Runner, he presented to me the pony which I had ridden on the buffalo hunt. I named him Runner.

CHAPTER III

It was the intention of Williams to strike for the South Platte River, in the vicinity of Laramie River, where he expected to meet with fur buyers, who would be returning to Green River; and either to dispose of our furs or have them forwarded to St. Louis, which at that time was the principal fur-buying city in the United States.

A few days' travel brought us to the South Platte River, and at a point fifteen miles east of Laramie River we found a Sioux village. Big Thunder was the chief, and he requested us to camp as his people wanted to trade. The Sioux were friendly in those days, especially to traders and trappers, and we had a royal time.

Just before daylight the following morning, an alarm was given in the village and all the men hurried out, to find that the Pawnees— mortal enemies of the Sioux—had run off about one hundred head of ponies which had been turned out to graze a short distance from camp. The number included two mules and three ponies belonging to our outfit.

As soon as the news was received, fifty young warriors hastened to saddle their best ponies. Williams signified his intention of going, but I told him that he was too old, and that Noble and myself would go and bring back the stock.

We started with the Indians, under the leadership of Young Thunder, a fine specimen of a coming chief. I rode my pony Runner.

We soon struck the trail of the Pawnees and followed it down the south side about ten miles, and then crossed to the north side of the river. We could tell by the appearance of the trail that they were only a short distance ahead of us.

The Sioux now discarded all their clothing, excepting leggings and breech-clouts, and mounted their war-horses, which had up to this point been led.

I put a pad on my Runner. These pads are made by filling two sacks with antelope hair. The sacks are generally made of buckskin, are seven or eight inches in diameter, and rest on each side of the horse's backbone, being sewed together on top with buckskin. Material is fastened to each side for stirrups and cinch. They would be a curiosity in the East, but are light and elastic, and a horse feels no inconvenience from them and can travel twenty miles farther in a day than under a saddle.

We started at a canter, Young Thunder in the lead. After going about eight miles, we noticed that sand was still sliding in the hoof tracks ahead. This was a sure indication that the Pawnees were but a short distance in advance. We now went at about half speed, the Indians becoming alert.

Passing over a divide we could plainly see a cloud of dust about two miles in advance. At about the same time the Pawnees must have discovered us, for there appeared a scattering just as if stock was being urged to greater speed.

We gained rapidly on the Pawnees, and were soon close enough to determine that the party consisted of twelve. They were trying their best to get the herd to a cottonwood grove on a bend of the Platte River.

It was at this time that I discovered the wonderful endurance of the Indian pony. Young Thunder gave a war-whoop, which was the signal for a charge. The ponies bounded forward as an engine when the throttle is thrown wide open.

The Pawnees heard the yell and left the herd of stolen stock and made for the grove, frantically urging their ponies to greater speed. Two of them went to sleep before they reached cover, ten getting safely to the grove, thankful of saving their lives, knowing that the Sioux would be satisfied with the two scalps and the recaptured herd.

Several of the ponies were close to the grove, and Noble and I dashed at full speed and turned them away. The Pawnees fired several shots at us, but the bullets went wide of their mark. As we were within one hundred yards of the timber, I wheeled and shot, but it was a waste of ammunition, as no Indians were in sight.

When we returned to our party, they had the two Pawnees stripped and scalped. I asked the Sioux if they did not intend to charge the Pawnees in the grove. Young Thunder, who had been a close observer of our actions in recovering the ponies, smiled, and shook us by the hand.

It is a question in my mind if the Sioux would have recovered these ponies but for us. They will not approach a solid body of timber with a heavy growth of underbrush. I thought then that Indians were not such terrible fighters as some writers made them appear; and my first impressions have never changed, although I have contended against some who apparently knew no fear, but they are exceptions.

We reached the village in due season, Young Thunder leading the party, the warriors following singing scalp songs and carrying the Pawnee scalps tied on the end of "coup" sticks. The whole village turned out to greet us, and all were yelling like furies. They could tell by the song of the warriors that no loss nor damage had been sustained, which is not always the case.

16

Pandemonium reigned all night, with singing and dancing and the re-counting of the warriors' bravery in taking two scalps and recapturing the ponies stolen by those "dogs of Pawnees."

When Williams heard of my going close to the timber, he said: "I shall have to keep you at home next time, if I expect to return you to your parents. You are a young fool to approach close to timber where hostile Indians are concealed."

I told Williams that three of our ponies were in the bunch and that I did not want to return without them. I thought the Sioux were cowards, but I have learned by experience since that a white man, on the plains at least, will risk where an Indian dreads.

The Pawnees had not acted with good judgment in trying to drive off one hundred head of horses so near daylight. They should have realized that the Sioux would be on their trail in a short while, mounted on their best horses.

Indians are credited with being extraordinarily cunning in stealing horses, the Pawnees especially so, which is the reason other tribes call them "Wolf Indians." The sign for wolf is the index finger and thumb spread apart, other three fingers ends to palm, the hand held up to the side of the head. This is the uniform sign both for wolf and for Pawnee.

I have made mention of coup-sticks. While all tribes do not call it by the name "coup," the custom and usages of all are identical. These sticks are generally made of willow, and are from seven to ten feet in length and one inch in diameter. The bark is peeled and they are painted with vermilion, after the fashion of barbers' poles. Warriors invariably carry these sticks in action, and when a foe falls the one who strikes him with a stick claims the "coup," or one brave action done. A brave's valor is determined by the num-ber of "coups" he has to his credit. Sometimes a half dozen Indians strike the same foe, and each one claims a coup and is entitled to and gets part of the scalp.

CHAPTER IV

We started the next day for the Laramie River, where we expected to visit another Sioux village, whose chief was Black Moon; also to meet some traders from Green River, men representing the Northwest Territory Company, and some opposition traders. There existed great rivalry among them to secure their furs and robes from "free trappers," as our outfit was classed. Corporate companies were not friendly to free traders and trappers, and made it very unpleasant for them when opportunity offered. In those days the cream of men in the mountains belonged to the free traders and trappers, and it followed that corporations had no "walk away," as mountain phrase had it.

The Sioux were very wealthy from an Indian standpoint, owning vast numbers of horses and mules and furs and robes and they were generally considered "nabobs." They roamed the plains with their villages, so as to be in close proximity to buffalo, of which they required large numbers, as meat was their principal food, and sent out war-parties against their enemies, who were numerous and included Pawnees, Crows, Utes, and Iowas.

So it followed that they kept constantly on the go, and for recreation, when a war-party had returned from a successful raid, bringing back scalps and ponies, all women related to the party would decorate themselves in all their barbaric finery and promenade through the village singing and chanting the bravery of their lovers and husbands, and making all the other women in the village feel abashed. This is the secret spring of war-parties constantly going out. The singing, dancing, and feasting are continued several nights and days. Very different are the conditions when war-parties return defeated. A gloom is cast over the village. Relatives of those who are slain or are missing cut off fingers and in other ways mutilate themselves; and a council is held by the medicine men to devise some plan by which they may get revenge on the enemy. Bear in mind—and this is true of all tribes, notwithstanding contrary statements by some writers who have had no general knowledge of the character of the Indian, either on the plains or in the mountains—an Indian never for a moment considers himself the aggressor. Sufficient for him is the fact that some member of the village has been lost.

We reached Black Moon's village on the Laramie River the next day, camping near the chief's lodge.

The story of our recovering the stock and the taking of two Pawnee scalps had preceded us, and the young warriors wanted to see the young paleface who had ridden close to the grove. They looked upon that as a great feat, though I failed to see it in any such light. As it was, it made me many friends among the young men. The older ones, however, said that I was a young fool and would lose my scalp some day.

We traded for considerable fur at this camp, which somewhat astonished Williams, as there were three traders on the Platte River. The reason was, as I have already stated, that the traders were not up to their business in such ways as paying uniform prices for furs of the same quality.

A war-party of young men came into camp that night from the Sweetwater River and informed us that a trader with wagons would be along the next day.

The next morning we unpacked all our furs, classifying and rebaling them. Williams took great pains to instruct me in all this, saying that he intended to make me the equal of anyone in the business, as it might be useful in later years. I often think that he had a presentiment that I would never return to civilization.

In the afternoon an old trader named Vasques arrived with wagons and oxen, and was astonished to see all the furs we had collected. He looked surly, but this did not worry Williams, who understood his disposition. Williams should have been engaged by the government as a diplomat, for he could outwit any and all of these arrogant corporate traders.

At any rate, Vasques saw that his only chance to get furs and robes was to curb his temper and come to terms, which he did, paying us $750 in cash for the beaver and other small furs, and a quantity of Indian goods, of which he had a fine assortment, for the robes.

Williams got the best of him on every turn. He either had to trade with us or haul his Indian goods back to the States, which he was not inclined to do.

When departing the next day, Vasques said that he would make this business of free trading most interesting for all concerned. I admired Williams's reply, which was, "Good, Mr. Vasques; remember I will be on hand to take an active part in the matter when it occurs."

We now had fourteen pack-horses, loaded with a fine assortment of Indian goods, and moved up the Platte River to the mouth of the Sweetwater.

While making camp six young Arapahoes put in an appearance and told us that their village was a short distance up the Platte River. It consisted of one hundred lodges, with Yellow Bear as chief. This was old Yellow Bear, father of the one killed on Sand Creek by Colonel Chivington.

Williams rode back with the Indians to their village. His object was to have the Indians bring their robes and furs to our camp, as we intended making a long detour before reaching Green River. Yellow Bear and his son returned with him to inspect our goods, and, being satisfied, returned to the village. We stood guard that night, as we were in a country dangerous from outside war-parties.

The next morning the village arrived early. They were wild-looking Indians, and not to be trusted. They were a thieving outfit, as the whites found out in after years.

Trade opened at once, and by noon we had one hundred robes and a quantity of other furs. Then came a feast and a smoke with the chiefs, after which they all returned to their village.

We hurried in packing up, for Williams wanted to reach the Independence Rock crossing of Sweetwater River as soon as possible. He was in hope of meeting another wagon outfit that might be coming from Green River, and to which we might dispose of our furs. We reached the crossing the next day at noon, but found only Vasques's wagon trail.

It was while at this camp that I had my first introduction to Crow Indians, when Williams halted a war-party, or, more properly speaking, a thieving party of twenty-three, within fifty yards of camp. We had all our packs placed in a square, the robes making a fine breastwork.

The Crows were very insolent and came very near bringing on a fight. In the first place, they wanted a feast. Then our best horses, giving in exchange poor ones. They also demanded blankets and furs, all of which Williams gave them to understand they could not have. They next wanted to examine our outfit and trade, but Williams knew that they had nothing to trade and he told them so, and also advised them to leave. At this they became more insulting.

We had two large, shotguns which we used on guard at night, as they were most effective weapons at close range, being loaded with a half-ounce ball and five buckshot. One tall Indian, diabolically painted, stepped towards where I was standing and I brought my gun to bear upon him. At this he said, "Mas-to-shera mo-mo-nar-ka," and retreated. Perkins told me that meant, "White man fool."

Finally the Crows asked for some tobacco, which Williams gave them with the understanding that they were to leave at once, and they did, casting in sign to us, "Mean white men," all of which I understood.

I felt very much like resenting, but was restrained by Williams, who said that I must not heed such things from Indians. After many years of experience I fully agree with him.

We remained in this camp two days and then started for the upper Wind River country, hoping to meet the Shoshones, who frequently remained in that section until May, furs still being in their prime. It is amusing to hear men from the East claim that beaver and otter are only trapped in the winter. Such is not the case, as beaver and otter trapped in April and May are classed A1. I have sold to expert fur buyers furs trapped in June, and these same buyers credited themselves with being able to tell, by the appearance of the fur, in just what month in the year the furs were trapped.

On our third day's travel we met a trader named Pomeroy, who had Indian goods on hand, expecting to trade with the Indians on the trip to the States. Williams told him that all the Indians he would be liable to meet were without furs, which was stretching it somewhat. We then unpacked our furs and robes and offered to trade for cash or goods. It required half a day to consummate the trade, we receiving $300 in cash and a quantity of Indian goods. Williams told me afterwards that Pomeroy would not make much on that trade. I think that Williams must have hypnotized Pomeroy, as he overlooked the important fact that at this season of the year Indians were still dressing robes and would continue to do so for six weeks to come, and Pomeroy would have had plenty of opportunities to trade with villages on his way down Platte River. But Williams made him believe that the villages were leaving for buffalo, which was not so, as they had an abundance of meat and buffalo were close by.

Williams was the soul of honor, and when I questioned him about his statements to Pomeroy, he smiled and said, "Diplomacy." I have never forgotten that, and after years of observation I find that honorable merchants follow the same tactics. Self-interest predominates among all, from the highest to the lowest. They evade the literal truth, calling their conduct "business diplomacy."

CHAPTER V

We continued on towards Little Wind River and crossed a most rugged and romantic country, whose lofty sky-piercing peaks ascended to and above the clouds. On the northwest were the Wind River Mountains, which are the main Rockies; to the eastward the Big Horn Mountains, world renowned in their isolated grandeur;—the home of all noble game, such as buffalo, elk, antelope, deer, and bear. It is a hunter's paradise. Here the different tribes of Indians met on their annual hunt, and the meet was often the scene of conflict.

We saw no Indian sign until we reached Little Wind River, where Evans and Russell picked up a moccasin. This was dangerous country. Hostile war-parties were numerous, and were liable to make their appearance at almost any hour of day or night.

Williams selected a strong position for camp, as he considered this the most dangerous country on the plains, being constantly invaded by war-parties of Blackfeet, Bloods, Piegans, and Crows. The trappers and Shoshones were kept constantly on the alert, to avoid losing their stock and even their scalps. Williams was of the opinion that the tracks discovered were made by a party of Blackfeet, as they almost always went to war on foot.

Beaver and otter seemed plentiful, and the men set traps. That night we slept with arms by our side ready for instant action; and kept close guard, as it was almost a certainty that the Indians had discovered us and would try for our stock. Noble and I stood first guard, and Evans and Russell second.

About four o'clock in the morning two shots brought us all to our feet. Immediately after the shots we heard yell after yell from the Indians, and they began firing at the camp with guns and bows and arrows. Evans and Russell had killed two Indians with their first shots. We fired at the flashes of the Indian guns; these were Hudson Bay flint-locks and made a very decided flash when discharged. The weapon is not over-effective, but will do damage at short range. Some of our shots must have taken effect, as the Indians fell back, though they continued sending shots to camp until close to daylight.

Several of our men, myself included, wanted to charge, but Williams would not allow it, as he considered it dangerous charging an unknown number of Indians at night, although he had concluded that there were not more than a dozen in number, if so many.

Just before daylight the Indians attempted to recover their slain comrades. They are expert in crawling through grass, but our men were up to all their tactics and prevented them and added one more to keep company with the two already sent to their happy hunting-grounds. The Indians gave a yell of despair and departed, sending after us a few parting shots.

Daylight was now appearing in the east and objects could be seen at a distance. Noble and Russell "lifted the hair" of the three dead Indians, and as they had had some experience in scalping it was easily accomplished. The method of scalping was to run the knife around the head under the hair, cutting through to the skull bone; then taking hold of the scalp-lock and giving it a quick jerk, the scalp would come off and was afterwards dried on a hoop.

The reason that mountaineers scalped Indians was in retaliation, and also because Indians dread going to their happy hunting grounds without their scalps. For this reason they will risk a great deal to get their slain after a battle.

We discovered a trail of blood leading down the river, from the place where they had fired the shots into camp, showing that some of our return shots had been effective. Five of our ponies had been wounded, one so severely that we killed him to put him out of misery. Williams, enraged at the injury that had been done, was determined to punish the Indians still further. Leaving two men in camp he ordered the rest to follow him.

The experienced mountain man is as keen as an Indian on a trail, and no difficulty was found in following this one.

About five miles down the river a small stream put in from the north side. This stream was about two miles in length, and at its head was a spring surrounded by a small grove of quaking aspens. The Indians had gone up this stream, and we were soon close upon them.

Going at a rapid rate for nearly a mile, we came to a rise, and when on top we were within plain view of the Indians, who were hurrying along, trying to get two of their wounded comrades to the grove. They were about half a mile in advance of us. To keep them from reaching the grove, Williams dashed to the right, where there was a level bench or prairie, so as to give our horses a chance to go at top speed.

The Indians saw in a moment that they would be cut off from the grove, and they made for a patch of willows and stunted box-elders just below.

There were eleven of them, and we had them cornered, as trappers say.

From the brow of the hill on our side to the Indians in the willows it was about one hundred yards, and Docket tried a shot. The Indians returned fire, wounding him in the thigh. It was a flesh wound, but bled freely. As there were a quantity of boulders close by, Williams gave orders to roll them up to the brow of the hill for breastworks.

Leaving Evans, Russell, and Docket behind this breastwork, with orders to keep shooting at the Indians, Williams told Noble and me to follow him to the grove without letting the Indians notice our departure.

In the grove we cached ourselves, although I did not understand Williams's plan. Its wisdom was soon apparent.

The men on the brow of the hill kept up a steady fire, and the Indians realized that they would be annihilated if they remained in their present position.

Six of them made a dash for the grove, and when they came within one hundred yards Williams gave orders to shoot. We made a lucky shot, and three of them fell face down. The other three gave a yell of despair and ran up the hill. We mounted and dashed after them. The Indians were panic-stricken when they saw us so suddenly mounted.

I now saw what Williams was in a fight. Reckless to an extreme, he dashed at the Indians, who wheeled and shot but missed. A tall Indian was in advance and Williams made for him, and in a shorter time than it takes to write it, there were three more dead Indians. Williams had identified them as Blackfeet, and this was afterwards confirmed by the Shoshones when shown the scalps.

Williams now said: "Boy, this is your first opportunity. Lift the scalp from that buck. It belongs to you."

Of course I knew how to scalp, and soon accomplished the feat, much to his satisfaction, for he said, "You are broke in now. You will do."

Flattering, I thought, coming from such an old Indian fighter as he was. We went after the first three and then returned to the men at the breastwork and found them waiting for us. Many men would have left those five Indians in the willows, satisfied with the revenge. Not so with Williams.

Some of our men told me that he was considered the hardest man on the plains to down in a fight with the Indians. He was never known to quit when once started. It was a fight to a finish.

It struck me forcibly in this instance, when he replied to my question of what he was going to do. He looked at me peculiar like and said: "There are five Indians down there who shot at and insulted us. They shall have what they would have given us had they been successful in their attack. Boy, never, if possible, let an Indian escape who has once attacked you." I was receiving a practical lesson.

He now said: "I want one of you to go with me. The rest of you throw some shots at the Indians while we get to the gulch and approach them from below."

But these fearless trappers held Bill in too great estimation, and they all said, "Once, old chieftain, your orders will be disobeyed. We cannot afford to lose you."

Russell said, "Evans and I will undertake that job. You cover us."

Down they bounded to the gulch below. Both were quick on foot, with eyes like eagles. They had been in many desperate fights, and understood the danger of approaching Indians in ambush. A wounded Indian is a dangerous animal when approached by an enemy.

We kept up a steady fire until our men were seen to be close to the willows. Evans and Russell now shot and bounded forward, yelling like Indians.

We also rushed down. One wounded Indian had arrow in bow, ready to shoot, but he was not quick enough. In a very short time all was over.

We found in the plunder two fine rifles, ammunition, knives, and other articles belonging to trappers. Williams said that some small party of trappers had been surprised by these Blackfeet, and in a few days we found that such was the case.

After collecting all the plunder we returned to camp. When Perkins saw what we brought back he said, "Well done, chieftain! Blackfeet had better give you the go-by."

Williams smiled and answered, "No better than you would have done." Either one of these men would have died for the other.

As we were "wolfish"—a mountain phrase for hunger—we did ample justice to the feast which had been prepared.

The men then went to look after the traps, and as I wanted to know all about trapping I accompanied them. They made an excellent catch of beaver and reset the traps. I observed closely the manner of setting and baiting. This is done in different ways, according to the condition of the banks of the creek, the dams, the depth of water, and whether there is a muddy or gravelly bottom.

Trapping is a science only to be acquired through long practice. I am considered one of the best, yet I am constantly experimenting. "Medicine," which is of various kinds, may be good on one river or creek, but not effective on others.

To skin, flesh, and stretch beaver and otter is quite an art, in which many trappers never become proficient.

CHAPTER VI

We remained in this camp three days, and Williams was constantly on the lookout for Shoshones or trappers, climbing up on high knolls and using a spyglass. On the morning of the fourth day we moved down Little Wind River to where it forms a junction with Big Wind River, and saw no Indian signs.

There is here one of the grandest and most romantic warm springs to be found on this continent. It is situated on the south side of the Little Wind River, about nine miles from the mountains. Its mineral properties are unexcelled, and according to scientific men it is the equal of any spring in what is now known as the National Park. The spring is on the Shoshone reservation. I have been told that New York capitalists are willing to pay the government one million dollars for it. The country from Owl Creek range to the base of the Great Wind River Mountains is called warm land by the Indians.

We stayed in this camp two days, keeping a sharp lookout, especially for war-parties. Here I set my first traps for beaver and caught two and one foot out of three traps set, which made me feel very proud. In those days beaver brought from $8 to $16 a hide. Dark otter skins brought a good horse from the Indians, or $10 to $12 from traders.

We next moved up the river about twenty miles, scouting the country towards Owl Creek Mountains, but saw no fresh Indian sign.

Here was a beautiful and strong camp, which could repel an attack from any number of Indians. Williams said we would have to remain here until we met the Shoshones, or ascertained if they had left for Green River by some other route. They avoided the plains as much as possible on account of the numerous war-parties to be found there.

On the fourth day, at evening, a scouting party of Shoshones was discovered by Williams. I was with him and we were some distance from camp. Williams said, "Shoshones." I asked him how he could tell, and he answered that it was by the way they acted, which he said denoted that they were the advance-guard or scouts of a village. They always have scouts out when moving villages, so as to be prepared for enemies.

We galloped towards them, firing a shot. The Indians saw us and heard the shot and understood that we were friends. There were nine in the party; they were acquainted with Williams, and seemed really glad to meet him.

They asked him who I was, and were told that I was a friend from the States. They accompanied us back to camp, where we had a feast and a smoke.

Their curiosity was greatly excited on seeing our captured trinkets, and Williams recounted the whole circumstances of our trouble with the Blackfeet. They were the most excited Indians I have ever seen from that day to this. When shown the scalps, many of them yet stretched on hoops to dry, they jumped up and gave a ringing war-whoop.

These same Blackfeet had killed two trappers on Gray Bull Creek, and had gotten away with five horses.

Williams told the Shoshones that the Blackfeet who had attacked us had no horses. They answered that we had not seen all of them; and that they had stolen seven horses from their village. According to the Shoshones' statement the war-party had split, and there must have been about thirty of them in all. The other Blackfeet were around, they said, and it made them uneasy. They wanted us to pack up at once and join their village. Washakie, one of the most remarkable Indians, was their chief, and he was a great friend of the whites.

Williams told the Shoshones to return to their village, taking two of the Blackfeet scalps, and to notify Washakie that we were camped here and wanted to trade. They departed saying that their village would be with us the next day.

We scouted the country for quite a distance up the river, but saw nothing. It does not follow because one sees no Indians that none are about. It stood mountain men instead to be constantly on the alert, Indians or no Indians. Many a poor outfit has come to grief by not taking the mountaineers' advice.

We were not disturbed during the night, and in the morning put everything in order to receive Washakie and his village.

Williams told the men that they could have all the plunder captured from the Blackfeet, and that the Shoshones would pay good prices for it. He told me that I could get a good horse for my two scalps. Docket gave me a fancy scalp, saying, "Now, young chief, you can buy a squaw."

About three o'clock Washakie, with a bodyguard of twenty men, rode into camp. It was a pleasure to see that noted chief and Williams meet. Long-parted brothers could not have been more affectionate.

We soon had a feast prepared, and after the feast a smoke.

In the meantime the village made its appearance, and lodges were put up above and below our camp. We were, in fact, corralled.

The plunder was all spread on blankets, and as Indians are more acquisitive than whites, a lively trade sprung up, particularly with the women.

They would give a pair of fancy moccasins for almost anything that had belonged to the Blackfeet.

The chief's son brought a good horse and presented it to me. Any one acquainted with Indians knows that a present from them means that you own something that they want. I soon found out that it was the scalp he wanted and I gave it to him. He was a noble young man, with the characteristics of his father.

The Shoshones were delighted at my proficiency in sign-language, for by this time I was able to converse on any and all subjects.

It must have been very amusing to hear the many questions the women asked me. "What tribe had I been raised with?" "Where was my Woman?" "Had I left her?" They would not believe that this was my first experience.

Trade continued until dark. The Indians exchanged moccasins, beaver hides, mink, martin, and buffalo robes.

Williams bought all the furs and robes from our men, paying them cash. They had no interest in our stock of goods, but were paid to accompany us. Any furs which they caught in traps belonged to them. They were all old acquaintances of Williams and Perkins.

The Indians stood guard that night, and in fact every night while we were in this section. It stood them well in hand to do so. Kalispell Indians generally paid this country a visit every spring to take a few scalps and ponies. The Kalispells were enemies to all Indians on the plains. When they and Blackfeet war parties met there was sure to be a clash, and this happened frequently.

Williams and Perkins held council most all night, while scalp dances and war songs were being indulged in by all the young folks. It makes no difference with Indians whether they take the scalps or not, if only these had belonged to their enemies. I have heard people make statements to the contrary, but they knew not what they were speaking of. Hence many false ideas originate in the minds of many well informed Americans.

The next day Washakie gave orders to his people to bring their furs and robes and give a good trade to their friends. This they did to our satisfaction.

Two mounted parties were sent out scouting for enemies, and a few to bring in meat. One of the parties met three trappers who belonged to the outfit surprised by the Blackfeet. An account of the troubles of these men will well illustrate the risk taken by trappers in collecting furs in those early days and even thirty years later.

The two trappers killed were off some distance from camp looking after their traps, when Indians surprised and killed them. The other three heard the shots and hurried to camp to secure what horses they could; but the Indians were able to run off five head and also to capture the two rifles which we had retaken. Williams returned the rifles and knives to the three men.

They were nervy, these three. One was a Scotchman, one a Frenchman from St. Louis, and the third came from Kentucky.

They said that when they heard the shots, they were aware that their companions had been attacked, so they rushed for their horses, securing six, the Indians getting three besides the two belonging to their dead comrades. "Kentuck" said they had no opportunity to render assistance to their fellows as the Indians charged upon them. They were camped in a thick grove of cottonwoods, and had prepared a breastwork for just such an attack. The Indians kept at long range, knowing that if they approached trappers' guns some of them would come to grief. All Indians dreaded trappers when once brought to bay. Any tribe to-day will confirm this statement. A few shots were exchanged and then the Indians withdrew.

"Kentuck" was anxious to find out what had been done with the two trappers, so he climbed a high knoll and saw about thirty Indians making for the mountains, half of them mounted.

He then went down the gulch and found his two friends dead, scalped, and otherwise mutilated in a horrible manner. His eyes flashed when recounting the circumstances. The reader can well understand the just cause for trappers retaliating. Good for evil is hardly a trapper's creed when dealing with Indians.

After burying the men they packed up and started to join the Shoshones, knowing where they were camped, and intending to remain with them until they reached Green River. They now joined our party.

In their possession were six packs of beaver of eighty pounds each, worth $9 a pound, making a total of $43 20. There was good money in trapping, but the rewards hardly justified the risk.

I found the Scotchman and the Kentuckian well educated men. The latter presented me with a copy of Shakespeare and an ancient and modern history which he had in his pack.

We had an abundance of reading matter with us; old mountain men were all great readers. It was always amusing to me to hear people from the East speak of old mountaineers as semi-barbarians, when as a general rule they were the peers of the Easterners in general knowledge.

These three trappers had caught a beautiful white beaver, a fur which is very rare and valuable. This they presented to Williams and would take nothing in return, saying: "You keep this as a memento from us of the high esteem in which we hold you."

In the afternoon the other scouting party returned and reported that near Owl Creek Mountains they had had a fight with a war-party of Pend Oreilles, and that two of their number were slightly wounded.

These two appeared very proud of their wounds. All Indians have that weakness, showing their wounds to all and looking for smiles from their lady loves for their bravery.

CHAPTER VII

The Shoshones expected to remain in this camp for several days, to give their women an opportunity to finish dressing robes and drying meat.

The grass was good, timber was plentiful, and a few buffalo were on the prairie. To supply the camp with fresh meat and to scout for war parties would keep the young men busy, so Washakie said.

In the meantime the Indians were having a joyous time dancing over Blackfeet scalps. I passed the time in visiting all the lodges, and studying the habits and customs. I was becoming interested and had a desire to learn everything pertaining to Shoshones, so that I could ascertain the difference between them and other tribes that I might come in contact with.

The scouts kept reporting fresh Indian tracks, but no Indians. This brought about a council between the Shoshones and our party for the purpose of devising some plan to rid this section of war-parties. We had more than a passing interest in accomplishing this. Not that we feared the war-parties, but we wanted to collect furs without being constantly annoyed.

Williams was the leading spirit in the council. After much deliberation it was decided to form three parties of twenty-five each, who should operate in conjunction, some of our party to be in each of the three.

By daylight the following morning all were ready, and we silently left the village, taking the routes selected.

Our company of Shoshones, including Williams, went to Bull Lake, as it was a favorite place for war-parties. Indian tradition had it that the father of all buffaloes roamed around this lake. From the high knolls surrounding the water one could sweep the country for miles with the aid of a spy-glass, and could readily discover any Indian village or trapping outfit.

When we reached Bull Lake Creek, where it forms a junction with Big Wind River, we saw fresh pony tracks coming from the east side of Big Wind River and going up the creek. It was impossible to tell the number, as they travelled in single file.

Every foot of this section was known to the Shoshones, which was of great advantage. We went up the creek for about three quarters of a mile, when the country became rough. Three of the young men now dismounted, stripped, and went on ahead to scout, we holding their horses. When we received a signal from the scouts we would advance to the point explored.

It was just about this time that we heard shots from the east side of Wind River, and we felt certain that one of our parties had come in contact with hostiles.

Our scouts approached a high-timbered knoll and discovered a band of Indians running towards a high ridge, looking in the direction from which we had heard the shots. Our scouts returned on a run and mounted. Moonhavey, a noted chief and warrior, took the lead, keeping under cover so as not to be observed by the Indians on the ridge.

We continued on for half a mile and came to a crooked draw which headed up on the ridge. The chief wheeled and went up this draw for a quarter of a mile and halted.

Just ahead was a sharp bend, which when passed would bring us in full view of the Indians on the ridge.

The Shoshones stripped to breech-clouts in short order and mounted their runners. Moonhavey gave the signal for a charge and dashed around the curve.

Within two hundred yards were fourteen head of ponies under the care of two young men. They gave a warning cry to their comrades on the ridge, who fired several shots without effect as the range was too great.

With a furious yell the Shoshones charged on the two men, who tried their best to mount, but they were soon on their way to their happy hunting-grounds. The Indians on the ridge, seeing the two men fall, disappeared.

Our party divided, one going to the right and the other to the left, until about three hundred yards apart, when both parties started up the ridge.

Upon reaching the top, we saw the Indians about one quarter of a mile distant, making for Wind River, where cottonwood groves were visible. Once there they would be able to stand us off for some time and more than likely kill some of us.

The country was comparatively level to the river, with the exception of two steep draws, which we crossed at a run. If the war-party had used good judgment they would have taken possession of one of these draws, but their minds must have been set on the timber and river. The war-party next scattered, which was another blunder, as they must have realized that they could not reach the timber and that we outnumbered them two to one. They should have remained together and taken possession of some buffalo wallow, for there were plenty of these around. I fail to see the wonderful strategy with which Indians are credited. I had a quick eye and I observed every move of both parties.

When the Indians scattered they were about two hundred and fifty yards ahead, and if the scene that followed could have been reproduced on canvas it would have been worth a fortune. It was a scene that occurs only in actual warfare.

The Shoshones gave yell after yell, charging madly and most recklessly. The chief warned them to be careful, but they paid no attention to him, for in a case like this it is a great feat to take the first scalp, and the successful warrior is greatly praised in their village. His lady love guys the other girls, claiming her lover as the bravest of the brave, first among their enemies. I believe the same rule exists among paleface girls, when a lover has performed an heroic act.

The war-party dropped blankets and war sacks, which contained tobacco, pipes, moccasins, and other things, thinking that the Shoshones would stop and pick them up. But the Shoshones charged on, redoubling their yells.

It was a wild scene for a few moments, shots and arrows flying in every direction. Williams, Moonhavey and myself had the fleetest horses and reached the Indians first. Williams killed the first Indian, while Moonhavey and I both fired at the same time and both missed, which chagrined me greatly.

I dashed after a tall Indian, who had his arrow strung, passing him at a run. We both fired at the same time, his arrow lodging in the fleshy part of my horse's shoulder, which would have ruined him if the arrow had had force behind it, but the Indian was scared. My shot knocked him down, and I heard Williams yell out, "Well done, boy!" There were only three left and they were having a combat with a few young Shoshones who were doing poor execution. Some older men stepped in and put a quietus to any further fighting by sending the three to join their companions in the happy hunting-grounds.

After "lifting hair" and collecting plunder, we returned to where we had left the captured ponies. Seven of them belonged to the Shoshones, having been stolen by the Blackfeet. Five of them belonged to Kentucky's party, and there were two strange ones, which Moonhavey forced Williams and myself to accept.

The shots had ceased from the east, so the chief sent the wounded men to the village, and the rest of us started over towards where we supposed our second party was. We discovered them clustered together near a spring. One Shoshone was dying, having been shot through the lungs, and three others were wounded. They had come in contact with nine Blackfeet, who had taken possession of a rocky knoll and made a breastwork on it. The two opposing forces exchanged shots for some time without any apparent result, as fearless Evans remarked. Council was held, and it was agreed to charge the knoll from two sides.

Six Indians were left behind to cover the charge by continuous firing at the breastwork. With a yell and a rush the knoll was charged, and a quietus was put on those nine Blackfeet in short order.

Evans had his cheek split open with an arrow, and "Kentuck" received a slight wound in the left arm. Williams always carried a supply of court-plaster, lint, and bandages for such emergencies, and soon fixed up the men.

After dressing the Indians' wounds, we took two long poles and fastened one on each side of a gentle pony, lacing a pair of blankets to the poles. On this we put the dying Indian and set out for the village. The other wounded Indians rode ponies and, fool-like, were proud of their wounds.

We reached the village at three o'clock and were met by half the tribe, who wanted to ascertain the cause of our slow approach. And now there was a mixture of joy and sorrow blended together; the relatives of the dead man mourning and making the night hideous with dismal howls, others singing, yelling, and sending forth war-whoops, parading the village, and recounting in detail all the incidents pertaining to the fight and the extermination of those "dogs of Blackfeet."

CHAPTER VIII

The third party had not as yet returned. In going through the captured war-sacks we found two white men's scalps, which "Kentuck" recognized as belonging to his partners. He buried them, saying, "I am not acquainted with their relations, or I would send or take the scalps to them."

Williams assisted me in cutting the arrowpoint out of my horse's shoulder, and he soon recovered, which highly pleased me. He and I were greatly attached to each other, and I used to feed him sugar every day. Docket said that I gave him more sugar than the whole party used.

Williams would answer, "Let the boy alone, he will get over that in time." But I never did while I owned Runner. Sugar was then worth one dollar a pound.

"Scotty" and Russell were with the third party, and Washakie, with all the head men of the village, held a council with Williams and Perkins to talk over the situation.

They came to the conclusion that there were no more Blackfeet in the country, and that the third party had come in contact with Arapahoes, Crows, or Kalispells.

Washakie finally decided to dispatch half a dozen young men to scout the country as far as Owl Creek Mountains, a distance of twenty miles, and to return at once unless they discovered something which justified a further advance.

The party was led by the chief's oldest son, a brave and energetic young warrior, bearing a remarkable resemblance to his noted father. They left, leading their running horses, so that in case of emergency they could either fight or run as circumstances warranted.

In the afternoon of the next day the third party was seen slowly approaching, and it was evident that it included some wounded. The Indian women who had husbands or lovers in the party became most anxious. Some of the Indians with spy-glasses ran to high ground to count their number, and soon made out thirty-three, which was the full complement, including the six young scouts.

On the arrival of the party in the village it was found to contain six wounded, including "Scotty" and Russell. The former was shot through under the left collar-bone, and Russell had received a glancing shot in the scalp. "A close call," as Perkins remarked.

They had met a war-party of twenty Piegans on the summit of Owl Creek Mountains. Shots were exchanged with little damage, and the Shoshones finally charged the hill. It was during this charge that "Scotty" and Russell received their wounds. The Piegans retreated, leaving two of their number. The Shoshones followed them about twenty miles, keeping up a running fight until the Piegans got into a strong position; then they withdrew. On the way back they lifted the hair of three killed in the running fight and two killed on the hill. They also collected considerable plunder, including five good ponies, giving "Scotty" and Russell their share.

The leading chiefs now held a council, and decided that there were no more war-parties in that section. All the Indians were jubilant and they went about saying that now all their enemies would fear them. They calculated without their host, as the saying is. When what had taken place became known among the Blackfeet and Piegans, they would be sure to hold a great council and concoct some plan whereby they could revenge themselves upon those "dogs of Shoshones" for the loss of their brave warriors. As I previously stated, Indians never consider themselves the aggressors. It is enough that they have lost warriors.

That same day we wound up our trade with the village and began to pack up. Williams induced Washakie to take all our furs to Fort Bridger, as well as the six packs belonging to "Kentuck's" party. The Shoshones intended to go by the South Pass route, while we purposed to cross the mountains and follow down Green River, collecting furs and bear hides en route. Bear hides were still prime in the mountains and were valuable. On the second day we parted company with our friends, who urged us to stay.

By this time I was almost equal to the best sign-talker in the village. Bear in mind that not all Indians are good sign-talkers. Dunces among them are as common as among whites.

Washakie would look at me quizzically and ask me with what tribe I had been raised? He could not or would not believe that this was my first experience among Indians. He would say to Williams that I could ride a horse as well as any of his young men and was their equal in shooting; while in fact I was their superior with both rifle and pistol, thanks to my early training. I mystified and bewildered them by turning hand-springs. My health was splendid and I was surcharged with energy.

As we now had eleven in our party, we apprehended no more danger from war-parties, but traders and trappers never relaxed their vigilance in those days. He who did so often came to grief.

If asked to compare the horsemanship of the Cheyennes and the Shoshones, I should say that they were equally skillful. Both can accomplish the difficult feat of retaining their seat on a horse while life remains; and they are like a cat, tenacious of life.

When wounded they retain their seat by winding a hair rope around the horse's body; sometimes they put their legs under this rope, tight to the thighs; and sometimes bring the knees up so as to form an acute angle, the rope passing tight over the thighs and under the calf of the legs.

They can lie on the side of a horse in action, and if wounded will retain the seat until out of danger of enemies.

I have heard some men claim that an Indian could lie on the side of a horse and shoot under its neck with bow and arrow, without the use of pad, saddle, or rope! To my knowledge such is not the case. I have many times been in action with mounted Indians and I have never seen it accomplished.

An Indian dreads to use a rope when approaching trappers in a fortified position, or when brought to bay. Trappers will kill the horse first, and they are then sure to get the Indian.

As hunters and shots the Shoshones are superior to the Cheyennes, for the reason that they are more of a mountain Indian and hunt more small game.

The domestic habits of the Shoshones are commendable for Indians. They are clean, inclined to be proud, and think a great deal of their women and children. They like to see them well dressed as Indian dress goes. Many of them have more than one wife, but one of the wives is superior to the others, who do all the hard work, such as dressing robes, collecting fuel, and packing the horses. Take them as a whole, the Shoshones are a contented and hospitable tribe and, no doubt owing to Washakie's great influence, friends of the whites.

We remained two days at Bull Lake and caught many beaver. I was now becoming very successful in trapping, and caught as many as any of the outfit. Williams taught me to skin, flesh, and stretch, in all of which I soon became proficient. Furs indifferently handled always bring a low price on the market.

We next crossed the mountains to the west fork of Green River, and found furs in abundance. We also found black, brown, and silvertip bear, getting several fine hides.

I went with Perkins on my first bear hunt. We succeeded in coming upon two black bears and got within one hundred yards without the bears scenting us. Perkins told me which one to aim at, and we both fired at the same time. His bear made one forward jump and then rolled over. Mine fell forward, growling and trying to get up, but unable to do so. I put another shot in the bear's head to finish her. Of course, I felt very proud of my first bear, though in later years I learned that it was easier to kill a bear than an antelope, provided you know where to shoot it. You are sure to get any animal shot in the shoulder-blade, because they cannot travel.

It has often been said that bears are the most ferocious animals in protecting their young. Such a statement is false, as I have many times seen a she-bear run away from her young, which were picked up and carried away into captivity. The mountain lion, so much dreaded by many, is cowardly and is only dangerous when cornered. The great danger in bear hunting is when a wounded one gets into a thicket. In such instances a good bear dog is needed. We shot two more bears that day, making a load for a pack-horse.

Perkins said to me after supper that night: "Now, young man, I am going to give you a practical illustration of how to shoot not only bear, but all other four-legged animals." He pulled out one of the bears and took the hide off. Next he spread out the legs and put the bear on its belly. He then cut the ribs from the backbone, cut down the flank, and pulled down the sides, so as to give a view of the bear's internal organs. He then showed me where to shoot from any position that it was possible for the bear to be in, and told me particularly to note how low the vital parts lay.

I profited by that lesson and never forgot or deviated from it. I would advise all persons to do likewise with their first bear. I would also advise them never to go into a thicket after a wounded bear, and not to hunt bears at all unless they have confidence both in their rifles and their own nerves. Many men are used up by wounded bears through their own ignorance.

Our wounded men had by this time recovered sufficiently to take an active part in collecting furs. We caught a quantity of martin and a few fisher. The latter is classed as American sable, with a demand twenty times greater than the supply.

We remained in this camp on the west fork for six days, and then moved down-stream about twenty-five miles and camped in a most beautiful place: an ideal spot for the poet to become inspired with the beauty and grandeur of nature and to be awed by the lofty peaks which ascended above the clouds.

At this camp we made a great catch of bear, having piled up a lot of beaver carcasses to attract them. I became expert in bringing down bear with the first shot. The men were all fine shots. They could not be otherwise after such long experience. They often received great praise from people for their expertness with firearms, but no more than they merited, for an American mountaineer had no equal on the globe. It was necessary that they should be expert, for they carried their lives in their hands. At any moment they were liable to come in contact with roving war-parties, who were never known to fail to attack a trapping outfit if they dared. To be taken prisoner was to experience a death none desired. A slow fire is merciful beside other cruelties practiced by Indians. All mountain men were acquainted with these facts, and therefore it was impossible for an Indian to capture a scout or a trapper—and scouts were invariably trappers. They knew what would follow.

I have often been asked why we exposed ourselves to such danger? My answer has always been that there was a charm in the life of a free mountaineer from which one cannot free himself, after he once has fallen under its spell.

CHAPTER IX

We left this camp with regret and moved down the river about twenty miles. Here we saw pony tracks, but could not determine whether they were made by Indians or trappers. Selecting a favorable location for camp, we built corrals and turned loose most of the stock under guard, picketing half a dozen of our best horses in case of emergency.

Docket and I then mounted our horses and followed the pony tracks, receiving a caution from Williams to keep a sharp lookout. Docket was an experienced scout, well up in Indian strategy, and we apprehended little danger of being surprised by lurking savages. We followed the trail about six miles, and struck a creek which we followed northward about seven miles. Here we came in sight of a camp, which Docket pronounced to belong to trappers. Arrived there, we found seven free trappers, three of whom were acquainted with Docket. They were somewhat astonished at seeing us.

Two of their number were badly wounded, having been attacked about ten days previous, when they lost half their horses and some of their traps. The Indians had discovered their traps and raised (stolen) them. This often occurs. The outfit were very glad to meet us, as they were out of tobacco and ammunition. They said that they would move over to our camp the following day.

When asked if they knew what Indians had attacked them they said no, but they supposed that they were Blackfeet. This tribe was the last to be out in the spring, its war-parties going in every direction, even as far as Salt Lake Valley and beyond, as all old mountain men can attest. There is a Blackfoot fort on a bench overlooking the great hot springs, north of where Salt Lake City now stands. The fort is still preserved, I have been told, as a memento of the old days. At all events, I myself, as well as many others, bathed in the spring and saw the fort long before any Mormons had reached Salt Lake Valley.

Leaving the valley Docket and I went across country, keeping a good lookout for bears, of which many signs were visible. About three miles from the trappers' camp we discovered a she-bear with three cubs passing over a ridge. Hurrying to the ridge, we saw the bears about two hundred and fifty yards away, turning over rocks in a hollow. We dismounted and crept to within one hundred yards, when Docket said, "You kill the old one." Taking careful aim I placed the bullet within an inch of the spot aimed for. She bounded forward and rolled over, with blood rushing from mouth and nostrils. Docket shot a cub, the other two running around thoroughly bewildered. We both shot again, each one getting his cub.

We took the hide off the old one and packed the young ones to camp. At this season of the year a cub is the daintiest of food, and one which few mortals have an opportunity of partaking of at the present day.

The other men had shot four bears, besides making a good catch in the traps. We were kept busy dressing and stretching until dark.

We stood guard constantly—one man at a time, and left nothing to chance. Just because no Indian sign had been discovered, it did not follow that no Indians were about or in the vicinity. If they were, they would have heard the shooting and would be sure to hunt up the camp before morning.

The next day the trappers whom Docket and I had met arrived and camped close to us. They traded several beaver hides for articles they stood in need of. They were a sunburnt, hardy and brave-looking lot of men, with erect forms and fearless demeanor. All but the two wounded ones were acquainted with our outfit. These two belonged in Santa Fe.

We remained in this camp eight days, and as the trapping season was over started for Fort Bridger, travelling by easy stages.

Here we found many trappers and traders who were having a high time, gambling and drinking. Many trappers became hilarious, but not offensive. A strict law prevailed among mountain men embodied in a few words: "Take nothing which does not belong to you without the owner's consent." A man who committed an offence would be fined about all he possessed, besides being ostracized. Far better to be dead than in that condition. He would never be allowed in a trappers' camp. His act would in a short time be known throughout all the camps.

It was at this time that I became acquainted with many of the old mountain men, such as Bridger, Anderson, and the Baker brothers. A great many trappers, such as Carson and Bent, resorted to Las Vegas and Santa Fe. There was a great rivalry among fur buyers at those places. Prairie schooners were constantly hauling goods from Independence, Mo., to the two towns.

Fort Bridger is on Black's Fork, a tributary of Green River, a beautiful location. Henry's Fork and other streams tributary to the same river contain the purest of water and an abundance of trout. Timber was plenty and the grass excellent for stock. It was an ideal place for a camp for either trapper or Indian. Washakie was camped about three miles from Bridger. He had not stored our furs at the Fort, but had them in his village.

Pomeroy and Campbell, agents for the Northwest Fur Company, were at Bridger, anxious to buy furs. They were acquainted with Williams, but were not on very friendly terms. In fact, they were not friendly with any free trader or trapper, but were too shrewd to show the dislike too plainly. They were arrogant, having a desire to control the actions of free trappers to their own personal advantage, something which they never accomplished. They struck Williams at once for a trade, and we packed all our furs from the Indian village to our camp. I observed closely the dickerings and tricks of those fur buyers on one side and of Williams on the other. It took three days before the trade was consummated to Williams's satisfaction. Our men got Williams to handle their furs, as none of them were able to deal with these leeches of fur buyers. We had a few Indian goods left, so Williams traded for more to complete the assortment, as he expected later to meet the Utes and Navajos. Besides the Indian goods we received one thousand dollars in cash and three checks on St. Louis bankers.

I mailed my check to father and got scolded for so doing when I returned for a thirty days' visit a few years afterward. I also wrote him that I should not return in the spring. I had become infatuated with mountain life and was enjoying splendid health. I would not have foregone the same for all the wealth in the universe.

Like Vasques, these traders threatened to make it very unpleasant for Williams some day. But this did not in the least disturb him. Perkins told them that they had better look out for Williams, as he had more influence with Indians than any of the traders.

"Kentuck" sold his furs and went back to the States, promising to rejoin our party in the spring. "Scotty" remained with us. Altogether there were about sixty trappers at Bridger besides a few Hudson Bay men. The order of the day was drinking, gambling, horse-racing, and shooting-matches. I believe gambling is contagious, for I could not resist trying my luck at target-shooting at five dollars a shot. I won two hundred and thirty dollars, much to the disgust of many old-timers, who thought they had an easy thing of it with a "boy." Our men all backed me heavily.

During the evenings I used to listen to old trappers relating stories, and they interested me greatly. From an historical point of view one in particular is worth recording.

In the year 1839 a party of forty men started on an expedition up the Snake River. In the party were Ducharme, Louis Anderson, Jim and John Baker, Joe Power, L'Humphrie, and others. They passed Jackson's Lake, catching many beaver, and crossed the Continental Divide, following down the Upper Yellowstone —Elk—River to the Yellowstone Lake. They described accurately the lake, the hot springs at the upper end of the lake; Steamboat Springs on the south side; the lower end of the lake, Vinegar Creek, and Pelican Creek, where they caught large quantities of beaver and otter. They also told all about the sulphur mountain, the Yellowstone Falls, and the mud geysers, and explained the relations of all these more lucidly than any map can show them.

They also described a fight that they had with a large party of Piegan Indians at the lower end of the lake on the north side, and on a prairie of about half a mile in length. The trappers built a corral at the upper end of the prairie and fought desperately for two days, losing five men besides having many wounded. The trappers finally compelled the Piegans to leave, with the loss of many of their bravest warriors. After the wounded were able to travel, they took an Indian trail and struck a warm-spring creek. This they followed to the Madison River, which at that time was not known to the trappers.

I listened with rapt attention when they described the wonderful springs at the Lower Basin, especially the one situated on the bank of the river called Fire Hole. It was this spring which gave the name Fire Hole Basin.

The description of the geysers on the upper Madison River astonished all the trappers present, and Williams advised me to take notes, as he wanted to visit that section.

Many years after I guided a party through that country and it lay as a picture before me. I used to describe in advance what we should see from day to day, and members of the party said: "How comes it, Hamilton? You said that you had never been in this section before, yet you go from place to place describing everything just as it is."

In a very few words I enlightened them, and they thought it strange that the outside world had not earlier known about that wonderful country.

I gave them to understand that the outside world would not believe stories told by trappers of the grand and romantic scenery to be found in the Rocky Mountains. Had this wonderland been described in St. Louis in the early forties, the reply would invariably have been, "Old mountaineer's story." There is plenty of proof of this assertion. Trappers as a rule were an independent set when relating truths which were not believed. It was the fault of our advanced civilization that this wonderland was not brought to the notice of the general public years before it was.

Give me the man who has been raised among the grand things of nature! He cultivates truth, independence, and self-reliance. He has lofty thoughts and generous impulses. He is true to his friends and true to the flag of his country.

Many Shoshones were present at Fort Bridger, and they asked me all kinds of questions by signs, all of which I answered correctly, to the astonishment of old trappers. Even Bridger asked me where I had learned sign-language. I pointed to Williams and said, "From him." "Not so," said Bridger, "for you can teach him signs."

He asked Williams where I had come from and he was answered truthfully, but did not believe what he was told. Many old-timers thought I had been raised by some tribe. Even to-day people believe the same. Enough of this —it is sufficient to say that in one year from the time I started I was considered the most proficient in sign-language of all white men on the plains.

We stayed at Fort Bridger about two weeks and then, with Washakie and his Shoshones, moved to Brown's Hole on Green River, which is about sixty miles from Bridger and was a trappers' rendezvous. A few Utes and Navajos came up on their annual visit with the Shoshones, to trade and to race horses. These Indians collect considerable fur and are keen traders. We opened up our goods in a tent, and I was placed in charge as trader, having by this time a fair idea of the quality and price of furs.

CHAPTER X

We remained at Brown's Hole until the first of September, making several excursions to the Uintah Mountains, a beautiful and romantic country and then a hunters' paradise for small game.

Nothing occurred to mar the good feeling between the whites and the Indians. I spoke of this to Williams one day when the three tribes were parading on horseback. Indians and horses were decorated with paint and trappings of finery, according to the taste of the owner. Each man was trying to outdo the others in horsemanship, stopping ponies when in full career, halting at a mark, at a jump—the one who succeeded in stopping the nearest to the mark winning the trophy. I had seen Cheyennes and Sioux parade, but they were not equal to these.

The whites and Indians held shooting contests on horseback, and the former showed their superiority. Three posts were set in the ground, about twenty-five yards apart. They stood six feet out of the ground and were ten inches in diameter. The top of the post was squared for a distance of about twelve inches. The arms to be used were Golfs six-shooters. Horses were to be put at full speed, passing the posts not closer than ten feet, and the contestant was to fire two shots at each post.

Some of our party put two bullets in each post and all at least one. I tried it twice, and was somewhat surprised to find that the best I could do was to place one bullet in each post. The Indians had several pistols equal to ours, but only three of them hit each post, putting one shot in each. Many Indians hit but one post out of six shots.

With rifles the whites defeated the Indians still worse, shooting at all distances from twenty to three hundred yards. In those days the best rifles used were the Hawkins, and they carried three hundred and fifty yards. Wagers were always made, and the Indians always insisted that the whites should take first shot. Nine times out of ten the whites won, and then the Indians as an excuse would claim that "their medicine was not strong that day."

In riding bucking horses the whites also came out ahead, and it is well known to-day that the Indians never did equal them in this accomplishment.

I have already mentioned that two of our men were expert with bows and arrows. Russell was one, and Bowers, whom we called " Silver Tip," the other. They could hold their own against any of the Indians. In fact, we were all constantly practicing with them. Today I can shoot an arrow-point through an inch and a half plank.

Our party now started to get ready for the fall trapping season, which opened in the mountains on the 15th of September. Williams had to go to Santa Fe on business, but he promised to be back in the spring and organize a party for a two-years expedition.

He traded his mule, which was a good one, for a Navajo's blanket. The blankets are world-renowned. It is a question if any manufactured by civilized men are their equal. They are absolutely water-proof, and are made by the women entirely by hand. The colors are fast, and the secret of the art is known only to the Indians.

Williams presented me with his, and I kept it many years, making a serape of it. This is done by cutting a slit in the center large enough for the head to go through, and it will keep one perfectly dry in wet weather.

We traded all our furs to some buyers, taking in exchange sugar, coffee, salt, crackers, flour, ammunition, tobacco, knives, traps, etc., and cash, Perkins and myself taking the goods and Williams the cash.

The day before Williams started he took me for a walk and gave me advice in many things. He looked upon me as his son, and few fathers ever gave their sons better advice.

He also told me that he was writing a history of his life among the Pueblo, Navajo, and Apache Indians, and when completed he would give it to me, which he did many years afterward. I firmly believe that it was the only true history ever written of the characteristics, habits, and customs of these three tribes. In 1873 I was appointed United States Marshal, to look after some bad men and Indians at the Crow Indian Reservation on the Yellowstone River. Major F. D. Pease was agent at the time. For security I placed Williams's manuscript in the safe and three days later the Agency burned down. At the time of the fire I was on the trail of some cattle thieves, otherwise I would have saved a manuscript that can never be replaced.

CHAPTER XI

For the next ten days we were very busy getting into shape and organizing. Perkins was selected as leader. The party was made up of twenty trappers, and included our old men with "Scotty." A council was held on the 16th of September and it was decided to explore Salt Lake, Weber, Bear, and Malade rivers, and other streams, as circumstances and amount of furs should warrant.

The next day we started, a wild and motley looking outfit I thought. The Indians all crowded up to shake us by the hand and to warn us to look out for the Blackfeet.

Nothing of interest took place until we reached Weber River, which rises in the Wasatch Mountains and empties into Salt Lake. We followed the river down, passing through the canon, and came in sight of the Great Salt Lake Valley, spread out in all its primitive grandeur. I said to Perkins, "Here is a scene fit to be viewed by the gods." Perkins and the other men laughed, saying, "Bill is becoming poetical." It was no longer "Boy." "Bill" had taken its place.

Perkins wanted to visit a stream south of where Salt Lake City now stands, and on our way there we camped at the hot springs, noted before, taking a plunge or bath before the Mormons ever heard of that country. We also examined the Blackfoot fort on the bench overlooking the springs.

The next morning some Utah Indians called on us and wanted us to pay for being in their country. Such a thing could not be thought of for a moment. These Indians spoke the Shoshone tongue, which many of our men understood. They were also very fair sign-talkers. When informed that they would receive no pay, their chief, who was called Old Bear—and bear he was by his looks, for a more surly looking savage was never seen,—ordered us to leave immediately. He had with him some thirty warriors, who had a few flint-lock guns, bows and arrows, lances, knives, and tomahawks. They were thus fairly well armed, but by no means equal to our party.

Perkins, who was an expert in dealing with turbulent and insulting Indians, having great patience, tried by every means to pacify them and make friends, but without success. He made the Indians keep back from our outfit, and then they would spit at us and make signs meaning "dogs," which we all understood. I expected every minute to see the fight commence. We were prepared at every point, and our arms were in prime condition.

Perkins cautioned the men to have patience, for many of them were becoming nervous at the insults from the Indians. Trappers would not brook insults from any one, and as I saw these men grow more and more angry and bite their lips I thought it commendable in them to curb their feelings. All this time Perkins was trying his best to make peace. He filled his pipe, lit it, and offered it to the chief, who refused with contempt, saying, "Big Chief never smokes with white dogs."

Perkins's patience was now exhausted, and he told the chief in pretty plain language to get out. When the Indians saw our men prepare for action by standing in open order and bringing their guns down to bear on them, they mounted their ponies; and casting all kinds of insults at us, both in signs and in spoken language, they departed, going south, the very route that we wanted to take.

After they had disappeared we held a council, and Perkins thought that we would have to give up going any farther south, as their village was located somewhere in that direction. We were not afraid of the Indians, but we wanted to collect furs and would have no opportunity to do this without being greatly annoyed.

As things stood it was a certainty that the Indians would follow us, and that a fight could not be avoided. We concluded to take the back track, a thing that trappers seldom do, except under extreme conditions such as those just related.

The reader may be interested in knowing just how a company of twenty trappers divided the work in the business of collecting furs among hostile Indians.

In the first place, everything was held in common, which means that the value of all furs trapped was equally divided. All the men could not trap, for a picket had to be constantly on duty. A guard remained with the horses during the day. During the night the horses were corralled. One man had to take care of camp, and generally two men acted as skinners and caretakers of all the furs brought in. The remainder set traps, and all kept a sharp lookout for Indians. No shooting was allowed while setting traps, as a shot signified Indians, at which signal all were on the alert.

A general rule that was followed by all mountain men was to strap stay-chains or trace chains to the horses' fetlocks. It was impossible for them to stampede with such a fixing. When trappers lost their horses they were obliged to go to some rendezvous and restock, as furs could not be collected without horses.

We camped in a strong position on a sharp bend in the Weber River, where the banks were steep and the waters deep, so that in case of an attack the Indians could not approach from the river side. Perkins thought that the

Indians would undoubtedly hold a council in their village and concoct some plan whereby they could capture those "white dogs" and get all their horses. All this we understood, but, as I have said before, they calculated without their host, as the sequel will show.

Beaver signs were plentiful here, and after camp was made the men went out and set traps. At supper all hands were in camp.

We passed many jokes that evening, "Silver Tip" taking the lead, for he was by long odds the most humorous and comical member of the party.

Personally I was engaged in making a close study of all our men, particularly the new ones, and I came to the conclusion that they were a noble-looking body of men. With high foreheads and with calm and fearless eyes, their demeanor was that of gentlemen. I had read of Daniel Boone and Simon Kenton, and in my mind I began to make comparisons, wondering whether Boone or Kenton were any nobler looking than these men.

Then I thought of Leonidas and his handful of men repelling Xerxes and his immense Persian army. Could they be any braver or of finer metal than these trappers? As such thoughts passed through my mind, I came to the conclusion that the American nation might well feel proud of her mountaineers, who fearlessly explored the unknown wilderness, encountering and overcoming untold difficulties and dangers by the mere force of their own indomitable will-power and courage.

The true mountain men have never received the credit which they justly merited for their part in bringing this unknown country to light.

We only put up one ten-skin lodge for our effects, sleeping outside with arms in hand. Two guards were put on duty, to be relieved at midnight.

Perkins said that it was customary for the Utahs to attack just before daylight. It is at this time that Indians expect to find whites fast asleep.

A little before day two or three wolf howls were heard by the guards, who immediately notified Perkins, and he soon had all the men up. Our packs were placed in a semicircle as a breastwork, and twenty of our best horses were saddled and tied in a thicket, to protect them as much as possible from Indian bullets and arrows. About the only protection the Indians would have in approaching camp was the sage-brush which stood on the flat.

We had a fairly well-fortified position, and it stood us well in hand to have it so. The Indians, knowing our number, would attack us seven or eight to one, and perhaps more.

Trappers in those days were obliged always to contend against overwhelming numbers; but they never hesitated, and it was always a fight to win, for defeat meant death.

The first wolf howls were soon followed by others, coming from points nearer and in a semicircle. Indians are expert in imitating the cries of wolves or coyotes, and it is very hard to distinguish them from the cries of the real animals. On the other hand, even after years of practice, few whites can successfully imitate these animals. The hooting of the owl is frequently used as an Indian signal in attacking camps. All these signals are carefully studied by trappers and scouts, who are rarely deceived.

The Indians must have located our camp from the mountains, which were at no great distance, as our one lodge was set up in a cottonwood grove, which concealed it.

We had not long to wait before the attack commenced. Just at break of day the signals ceased, and the trappers knew that the crisis was at hand.

The Indians crept to within one hundred yards of camp before they gave the war-whoop. Then they came madly charging, fully one hundred in number.

The trappers had their rifles in hand and their pistols out of their scabbards ready for instant use after the rifles were discharged.

We let them get within fifty yards before delivering a shot, and at the discharge of the rifles many fell. Three of our men were armed with double-barreled shotguns, loaded with a half-ounce ball and five buckshot, deadly weapons at close quarters. These were now discharged and the Indians halted. Immediately the trappers began with their six-shooters, one in each hand, for as a result of long and constant practice they could shoot equally well with either. Every condition of his life obliged the trapper to be expert in the use of firearms.

At receiving so many shots from twenty men the Indians became panic-stricken. They had not calculated on the trappers having two pistols each— twelve shots apiece after the rifles were discharged. They had expected to exterminate us before we could reload our rifles.

The Indians retreated, assisting many of their wounded. Perkins had hard work to keep the men from charging, for our fighting blood was up. Had we charged, we would have lost several men, for the sage-brush was alive with Indians.

Several in our party received slight wounds, but none that were serious. An arrow went through my fur cap.

It was now getting daylight, and several wounded Indians lying close to our breastwork began shooting arrows at us, but our men soon quieted them.

When the sun was about two hours high, the Indians sent a messenger with a rag tied to a stick. Perkins met him outside. He said the Indians wished to make peace and that they had lost their chief, Old Bear, as well as many of their bravest warriors.

This was merely a sham. All they wanted was to save their slain from being scalped.

Perkins told the Indian to remain outside until he held council with his men. He was quite a diplomat, and made a strong speech to the effect that it would be best to make peace. It would certainly be to our advantage in collecting furs. The Indians had received a repulse which they had not expected. They would now return to their village, taking their dead and wounded, and mourn for many days. This would give us time to trap the Malade River and other streams before they got through mourning.

A vote was taken and resulted in seven wanting to continue the fight and thirteen declaring for peace. We did not fear the Indians, but we wanted to collect furs, not to fight. Perkins told the Indian to go back and bring five of his comrades to our camp.

In the meantime we cooked breakfast, keeping a sharp lookout all the while, for under no conditions do trappers trust Indians after a fight.

We did not have long to wait for the six Indians, who came up looking crestfallen at their failure. Perkins smoked with them and gave them some, tobacco. He then told them that if they molested us any more or stole any of our horses he and his men would wipe out their village.

"Big talk," Docket said; "twenty men wiping out six hundred."

However, they appeared mighty glad to get possession of their dead and they made signals to other Indians to bring up ponies, and they soon had the dead lashed to the ponies and departed. I counted thirty-two, which rather surprised us, as we had thought the execution very much greater. Had they attacked camp a half-hour later, in the same manner, their loss would have been doubled.

The next year we learned that many of the wounded had died, and that the Utahs declared that they had lost many of their best warriors. This tribe had frequently robbed small parties of trappers, many times killing them, and this was the first severe lesson that they had ever received. After this occurrence they invariably gave the well-organized bodies of trappers the "go by."

If any reader of this should doubt the fighting quality of the trapper, let him go among any tribe of Indians to-day and ask them what they think of it. They will invariably answer that it "costs too much blood to fight trappers."

This band was of the same Indians that gave the Mormons so much trouble a few years later.

CHAPTER XII

We finished our trapping in this section without being molested further, and then moved to Bear River. At this camp we came in contact with the Bannocks, whose chief was named Pocatello. It was he who fought Connor and his California volunteers in 1862. The result of the fight was that the Bannocks were simply annihilated. Pocatello escaped by swimming down the Bear River with the thermometer at 380 below zero, unusually cold for that country.

These Bannocks made annual visits to the plains after buffalo, and were expert in the making of pemmican. They were also adept in collecting fine furs, more expert than any other tribe I have ever known.

It was now October and furs were beginning to get prime. We trapped Bear River and Malade River with good success; and then crossed Goose Creek Mountains and trapped Goose Creek and Raft River.

Here we met some Pah Utes, a branch of the Shoshones, but the Shoshones do not affiliate with them. They were a primitive race, making fire by friction between two sticks. We visited their village, as I wanted to see how they conducted their domestic affairs. They could not be compared to Sioux, Cheyennes, or Shoshones, for they were filthy in habits. Their cooking utensils were primitive in construction. For spoons they used the hoofs of elk and the horns of mountain sheep. They are credited with manufacturing pottery, but I visited many lodges and saw none. They had a few kettles, which appeared to me all they desired. Their arms consisted of bows and arrows and a few indifferent flint-lock guns. Many arrows were pointed with flint, which they poisoned by dipping the point in liver which had previously been poisoned with rattlesnake venom. I have heard that they extracted a poison from roots, but this I very much doubt.

They collect quantities of berries, and for meats they have deer, antelope, mountain sheep, jack-rabbits, and ground squirrels. The last two are evidently their favorite food, for I noticed large numbers of them hung up in the village. They hunt squirrels with blunt-pointed arrows. They are great beggars and thieves, and we caught them trying to steal our horses.

The streams were now beginning to freeze up, and we started for the Brown's Hole rendezvous, arriving there the latter part of November.

Several traders had come from the States with supplies, and there was quite a rivalry among them for our furs. Bovey & Company were the most liberal buyers, and we sold them the entire lot.

Besides the trappers there were at the rendezvous many Indians— Shoshones, Utes, and a few lodges of Navajos,—who came to exchange their pelts for whatever they stood in need of. Take it all in all, it was just such a crowd as would delight the student were he studying the characteristics of the mountaineer and the Indian. The days were given to horseracing, foot-racing, shooting-matches; and in the evening were heard the music of voice and drum and the sound of dancing. There was also an abundance of reading matter for those inclined in that direction.

Perkins had a fly-tent put up and made a counter out of dry-goods boxes, and then said: "Now, young man, you take charge of the store. You are the best sign-talker in the camp and can out-trade me. Besides, the Indians and trappers are all fond of you."

I was the youngest man in the camp and full of the Old Nick, the men would say, for I was continually playing some prank.

On January 20th a fearful storm began, which raged for six days, scattering most of the horses in the hills, and made both trappers and Indians uneasy, as Blackfeet, Bloods, or Piegans were often in this section at this time of the year. These tribes are winter Indians, and storms and severe weather do not affect them in the least.

On the seventh day the storm abated, and about seventy-five trappers and Indians started out to gather stock. All our horses except six were missing. Among the six was my Runner, and mounting him I joined one of the parties composed of twenty whites and five Indians.

At Cedar Creek we struck fresh tracks of a large number of horses making due east to a comparatively level country. The Indians said to me in signs, "Blackfeet." We travelled at half speed for the next twelve miles and came to a ridge, from the summit of which we could see some Indians driving horses about one and a half miles away.

A draw to our right led towards the spot, so we turned up and at a rapid pace followed it to its head without being discovered by the Blackfeet.

When we reached the head of the draw, a Shoshone dismounted and crept to the brow of the hill and discovered the Blackfeet going over a hill beyond. Watching until they disappeared behind the hill, he signaled and we hurried forward to the next ridge.

From this ridge we could plainly see them and counted eleven. They had just halted to change horses, and when they caught sight of us they hurried to remount.

Our horses were the swiftest and we soon overtook them. They had no possible chance of escaping, and getting rattled they separated, which was just what we wanted them to do. Had they stayed together and fought they might have done some damage. As it was, they became panic-stricken at our sudden appearance. Here was a practical illustration of the efficiency of pistol practice at stumps. The trappers did not for a moment hesitate to charge the scattered Blackfeet; but each one selected his man and passed at full speed, delivering pistol shots at from twenty to forty feet distant.

Almost every shot brought down an Indian, who in the meanwhile attempted to fight with his arrows. In less than three minutes there were eleven dead Indians.

There was one Blackfoot mounted on a pinto pony who was leading the others, and as my Runner was the swiftest horse in our outfit the men yelled, "Bill, catch that pinto with that devil of yours."

The Indian at this time was two hundred yards distant, and I headed for him, and it was a grand race for a quarter of a mile.

I then spoke to my pony—"Catch him." He needed no whip nor spur, and I never saw him do better. When within fifty feet the Indian wheeled and let fly an arrow, but Runner would spring to the right or left by pressure of my knee and the arrow flew harmlessly by. Before the Blackfoot could fit another arrow to the string I was close to him and had sent him to join his companions.

We let the Shoshones do the hair-lifting, but we appropriated the plunder, which consisted of pipes, tobacco, and pemmican. The pemmican was pounced upon by all, as we were good and hungry. "Silver Tip" had received a glancing arrow in the ribs, but it was only a slight wound.

The trappers and Indians gave me the pinto pony, and it was a good one; it was very fast and had originally belonged to the Utes.

We then started for camp, having recovered one hundred and fifteen head of horses and mules.

The five Indians rode through their village with the scalps tied on coupsticks, and there was great rejoicing. They had had no hand whatever in killing the Blackfeet, but that did not matter. They recounted their bravery in recapturing the ponies and taking each one a Blackfoot scalp. We came in for no praise whatever from the women, as they considered that we were only assisting their brave young warriors. The dancing and feasting over this affair lasted for several days.

The Utes, on hearing of my catching the pinto pony, crowded around to see my Runner and after looking him all over challenged me to a race. I was to ride against the owner of the pinto. Of course I accepted and the bet was made, I on my part putting up a mule. The trappers and Shoshones all backed me and put up blankets, robes, and ponies. The track was selected, the word was given, and off we started.

Up to within one hundred feet of the finish we raced neck and neck, but I was holding my horse in and the little imp was mad. When I finally gave him his head, he distanced the Ute by twenty feet, much to his disgust. When Indians lose they give up gracefully, and no exception was made in this case.

It was now time to lay in a supply of depuyer and pemmican for spring, and about thirty trappers went to North Park and secured all the buffalo required. This kept all the outfits busy for some time.

CHAPTER XIII

In the early spring a trapper named Duranger, who had formerly been with the Hudson Bay Company, reached the rendezvous. He had come from the Walla Walla country, and reported that the streams flowing from the Blue Mountains contained large quantities of beaver.

About the same time, March 15th, "Kentuck" returned, accompanied by ten trappers from St. Louis. They brought all the late papers.

Five days later Williams arrived from Santa Fe, and a council was held to select some new field for collecting furs. Williams said that he had many times contemplated a visit to the country described by Duranger, and he made a proposition that as the year was 1843 we should form a company of forty-three men and make all preparations for a two-years trip. This was agreed upon and the trip lasted a little over two years.

Williams, Perkins, and I packed five horses with Indian goods, and the expedition started on the 25th of March, with everything in prime condition.

We travelled to Snake River and thence to Blackfoot River, where we met a Bannock village, of whose chief, Tygee, so much has been written. He was acquainted with many in our outfit and was friendly. We traded with him for a few furs.

Our outfit consisted of four different parties, who collected furs in common, that is, each one had an equal share in all furs caught by their own party. We had thirteen in our mess—an unlucky number you will say; but in this instance it proved quite the reverse. For mutual protection we always pitched our tents and lodges together. Each mess furnished its quota of guards.

Before proceeding further, it will be necessary to explain about the northern Indians who were so troublesome to the old-time trappers. Three tribes, Blackfeet, Bloods, and Piegans, make up what has always been known as the Blackfoot nation. The Piegan and Blood Indians claimed and occupied the country from the British line, 490 north latitude, to the Musselshell River on the south; and west along the summit of the Rocky Mountains to a range enclosing what is now known as Prickly Pear Valley, where Helena, Montana, is now. This represented a large area, and was commonly called "Blackfoot country." In the aggregate these Indians were numerous, and they were constantly on the war-path against all other Indians and all whites.

The third branch of the Blackfeet resided in and claimed the country from the British line to Fort Edmonton on the Saskatchewan River. Hence when a war-party of these northern Indians were met with they were pronounced "Blackfeet."

Many people even to this day believe the Comanches to be a tribe distinct from others. It is not so, for they belong to the Shoshone family, as do also the Utahs, Pah Utes, and Water-rickers, who principally lived on the Great American Desert or its border.

It must not be thought that trappers are an idle set while at the rendezvous. The reverse is true. Many of them are constantly dressing buckskin, and their mode of dressing is far superior to that of the Indians, as the skin when prepared by them will not stretch nor shrink when wet. Others are hunting deer, to keep the camp supplied with meat, or putting arms and traps in perfect condition. Most trappers make their own buckskin clothes, although there were two tailors at Brown's Hole.

Tygee told us that there were two parties of Hudson Bay trappers on these streams near his village, and that another party had gone up Snake River.

We held a council and decided to take the Boise River trail, as the Hudson Bay Company had a trading post in that section. We hurried along and reached the post with a few furs, which we traded to a gentlemanly old Scotchman who was in charge. He bought my pinto pony, paying me fifty dollars in cash. He told us that there were no trapping outfits in the Blue Mountains nor on the streams, but that the Howlack band of Bannocks were camped on Camas Prairie. This is known today as Grand Rond Valley in Oregon.

This band of Bannocks were not inclined to be friendly, and he advised us to cross the mountains to Walla Walla on the north side. This we did not care to do, as the streams between the post and Camas Prairie were full of beaver. We trapped all of them, and it was not until we reached Camas Prairie that we came in contact with the Bannocks. Here we ran on to their village of one hundred lodges.

The chief met us with a strong escort of painted and feathered warriors and commanded us to halt. This we did, not at his pleasure, but at our own. He asked us in signs what we were doing in his country, and in an insulting manner demanded several ponies. He also ordered us to unpack our goods, as he wished to see what we had. These demands we ignored.

The Bannocks were well up in sign-language and most of the chief's speech was understood by our men, all of it by myself. The chief was given to understand that he would receive no ponies, and that we would not unpack. If he wished to smoke and be friends, good. If not, he must get out of our way, as we were going on, and we claimed the right to trap in all streams either in the mountains or on the plains.

When the chief heard this he appeared to be thunder-struck.

The Bannocks had a great many Hudson Bay flint-locks, bows and arrows, and a few lances, mostly carried for ornament, but used also to spear a fallen foe.

Our men were becoming impatient and would have opened fight then and there had not Williams, who had been chosen leader, restrained them.

The chief saw the action of our men and realized that he stood on delicate ground. He withdrew in a threatening manner. But it was plain to all that we would see more of these Bannocks. Heretofore they had stripped and robbed many small trapping outfits, but ours was the first large company that had travelled through that country.

We passed by the village and continued some twelve miles, camping in a commanding position on a cottonwood creek. We built corrals and dug rifle-pits, as we felt positive that Howlack would resent what he considered an insult by following us with a strong war-party. All our band were old mountain veterans, with the exception of George Howard and myself. Howard was a brother of "Kentuck," and was over six feet tall.

A few traps were set, but not far from camp. Pickets kept a sharp lookout, and at sunset discovered a few Indians at a distance. They were locating our camp—a sure indication that mischief was intended.

Had Howlack seen the preparations we made to receive him he would have hesitated before attacking us. All our war-horses were saddled with pads. In fact, they were always saddled in readiness, but were never mounted except in case of emergency. Six men at a time stood guard, with three hours' relief.

At about four o'clock in the morning the guards fired several shots at wolves prowling in close vicinity to camp. Two of the wolves were shot in the head and proved to be Bannocks. Other wolves were seen departing.

Indians are very expert at this imitating the actions of wolves. Putting a large wolf hide on their backs and creeping on their hands and knees they imitate the wolf very closely. But mountain men are up to all such strategy, and many an Indian has come to grief while trying the game on trappers.

These warriors had been sent by the chief to ascertain the exact strength of our camp before he attacked in force.

When the guards shot, the rest of the men were all asleep with arms by their sides, ready for instant action. Before the smoke had cleared from the rifles all of us were at the breastworks.

For some time nothing more was seen of the Bannocks. We were certain that the guards had made no mistake, for they dragged in two Indians who had played wolf, and "lifted topknots," as "Kentuck" said. The chief must have been waiting for these two men to return and report, although by this time he must have concluded that they were either killed or wounded.

Just at daylight a strong force of mounted warriors was seen approaching. When at about three hundred yards from camp they halted and held a consultation. We estimated that the Indians numbered three hundred.

After a little about one half of them dismounted and made a flank movement, crossing the creek so as to attack us from two sides. On the creek side, opposite camp, was an open country, and we were well fortified. Williams detailed ten men to watch this side, and arranged so that they could be reinforced in a moment if necessary.

Strict orders were given to make every shot count. It demoralizes Indians when they see their comrades fall. A few determined men can stand off a great many Indians.

As soon as the foot Indians reached the opposite side of the creek they opened fire. Immediately the mounted Indians with yells and war-whoops began the charge.

We held our fire until the enemy were within seventy-five yards and then opened up. Almost every shot counted. Many Indians fell from their horses, and ponies fell pinning their riders.

Then seven double-barreled shotguns poured in their fire on the Indians, who had halted and were somewhat clustered. The shots created havoc and with a yell, as of despair, they fell back, leaving many wounded.

Thirty-three of our men mounted their warhorses and charged, but the Indians were excited and bewildered and broke for cover.

Our men with their deadly Colts told with terrible effect. We kept up the chase for about a mile, losing one man, a Virginian named Albert Smith, a brave man in every respect, and one whom we could ill afford to lose.

We captured sixty ponies and many flintlock guns. Each trapper had one scalp and some two, but they were dearly bought. Of our men one was dead and there were eleven wounded—four seriously, but all recovered.

Perkins's favorite horse had a broken leg and had to be shot. My horse was shot in the fleshy part of the thigh, but the wound did not interfere with his part in the action. Many of the trappers' horses had wounds.

I have been in many an Indian charge since this one, but I have never been in one that was so savagely executed. What made this one so bitter was that when Howlack went from our meeting on Camas Prairie he said in signs, "You white dogs, I will wipe you out."

As soon as the Indians who had attacked from the creek side saw the tide of battle sweep away their companions, they left their position, leaving eleven wounded.

We buried Smith in one of our rifle-pits so that the Indians should not find him. They will dig down ten feet to get a white man's scalp. We fooled them this time, for they never discovered Smith's body.

I saw Howlack in the lead of the retreating Bannocks and told Williams that I thought my horse could catch his, but he said to "Let him go."

This was the same band of Bannocks who, a few years later, annoyed the emigrants in Oregon. It was an unfriendly tribe and is not to be trusted even to-day.

CHAPTER XIV

We raised our traps and packed up to move camp, constructing four travois for those who were wounded. Duranger said we could reach the Umatilla River by sundown, and we did so.

In this section were to be found a tribe of Umatillas who had friendly inclinations toward trappers, and who were enemies of the Bannocks. We were soon discovered, and the chief, accompanied by a few braves, paid us a visit. He was over six feet tall and was a fine-looking Indian. The Hudson Bay men had christened him William Snook.

When we returned to Green River in 1845 the report of our fight with Howlack had spread all over that country, and we were asked many times why we had charged these Indians. They claimed that we had the Indians whipped before the charge and that we were secure in our camp. Our answer was that if we had not charged them, they would have annoyed us constantly, and we wanted to stop that and force them to respect the white men. The trappers felt confident of their ability to rout them, with little loss to themselves. The after results confirmed the wisdom of our course, for ever after that fight these Bannocks dreaded trappers. I have heard Hudson Bay men relate that when these Indians acted arrogantly, they would scare them by saying, "We will bring those trappers if you don't behave." The threat always had the effect of restraining them.

Indians will not stand a white man's charge. They dread close quarters and get bewildered. I have heard it claimed that the Indians can hold their own in hand-to-hand conflicts. The experiences of old mountain men do not show this to be the case. Fifty determined white men of experience can rout almost any number of Indians. I know that this is so.

Duranger could converse with the Umatillas in Chinook, and he told them of our fight with Howlack, showing the scalps and the bows and arrows. The chief became greatly excited and dispatched a runner to his village, and in a short while every Umatilla in the country appeared at our camp. They were the most excited lot of Indians I ever saw, and wanted us to move our camp to their village, as they were sure that Howlack would follow us to seek revenge for the loss of so many warriors.

We refused his kindness, declaring that we considered Howlack and his warriors as so many "old women." This was "big talk," but it had its effect.

These Indians had never seen so many scalps taken at one time, and they had never heard of such a thing.

They brought us an abundance of dried salmon and fresh deer meat and were very friendly.

The chief was a fair sign-talker, but he was somewhat astonished to see a smooth-faced boy who could excel him. He asked me what tribe I belonged to, or if I was a half-breed. Our men understood all this, and rallied me plenty about being a half-breed.

The chief had a fine horse which we wanted for Perkins, so we brought scalps and other things and laid them in a heap at the chief's feet, pointing to his horse. He understood in a moment and, taking the horse by the rope, passed it over to Williams, who in turn led it to Perkins. The old veteran was greatly pleased with the act, and the trappers were happy to be able to show the esteem in which he was held.

George Perkins, a native of Louisiana, merited all he received. He was brave and generous to a fault, and was ever on the alert for the interest of all.

We remained in this camp eight days and collected lots of furs, the Umatillas meanwhile keeping a sharp lookout for Bannocks, but seeing none.

On the ninth day our wounded men were able to ride, and we moved down the river to the base of the mountains. From a high knoll we could see the entire Walla Walla Valley, and it was a most beautiful panorama. The Umatillas also moved their village and camped three miles below us.

The fur season was now over and we took advantage of this opportunity to explore the country, remaining here two weeks.

Cayuse and Walla Walla Indians visited us. They were clean and somewhat proud, and very little addicted to begging. All these tribes were enemies to the Bannocks, who were constantly stealing their horses. The tribes owned large numbers of horses, and I have been asked where they got them from. Many years prior to this, the Indians had learned that there were great numbers of horses in southern California. Thereupon the Nez Perces, Yakimas, Cayuses, and others made up a strong war-party and went to the Sacramento Valley and returned with a vast herd. In later years, when I asked them, the Nez Perces confirmed this story.

The two weeks passed very pleasantly. Our time was spent in exploring, hunting, and fishing. Game was abundant on every side—deer, elk, mountain sheep; and we had all the fresh meat we wanted. The streams were full of trout.

The Indians were enjoying themselves to their hearts' content with their nightly scalp-dances. Williams and I remained in their village one night and I visited most of their lodges. They were neat, clean, and well furnished. The

Indians were hospitable to friends. They had an abundance to eat, such as camas root, none of which is produced far east of the Rocky Mountains, dried fish, meats, and berries.

They occupied a rich and beautiful country, and Williams in commenting on it, said, "The time is not far distant when this country will teem with life and the Indian will pass away."

Our men had now fully recovered and we were ready to go. Duranger said that there was a beautiful valley situated about one hundred miles west, which the Hudson Bay men called Tygh Valley.

We bade the Umatillas good-bye and went to Tygh Valley, expecting to remain there until furs should come in season, which would be about September 15th.

We travelled slowly and made many camps, stopping three days at a beautiful stream called John Day River to hunt and fish. We next moved to Des Chutes River, the fountain-head of which is the summit of the Sierra Range.

We crossed the river below the falls, which must have been about thirty feet in height. Here the Indians secure large quantities of salmon by spearing. Their spears are made of light pine, and are from seven to nine feet in length and about an inch and a half in diameter. The lower end is tapering, and is wrapped with linen. A spike about five inches in length, sharpened at the points and wrapped in the center with cloth, is fixed in a cavity of the shaft. The fisherman launches the shaft at the salmon, having a cord fastened at the upper end of the shaft and around his wrist. When the spike enters the fish the shaft is withdrawn, leaving the spike in the fish. They never fail to bring the fish to shore. They split the salmon open at the back and spread them on racks to dry in the sun for future use.

At the falls was camped a village of Indians, whom Duranger pronounced to be the Dog Creek tribe; they were friendly.

About seventy miles north of this place was a Hudson Bay trading-post, situated on the Columbia River. As we had collected a considerable stock of furs, we concluded to visit the trader and dispose of them. It was my first sight of the Columbia River, with its scenery beautiful beyond description. The trader was Dr. McLaughlin, a formal but courteous gentleman, who owned a large share in the Hudson Bay Company's lucrative business. We traded all our furs for cash and goods, and had to wait three days while a runner went to Vancouver, the Company's headquarters, for the cash.

The head men of the Hudson Bay Company did not look favorably on American trappers and traders. They claimed the right to collect all furs in a given area on the American side, having a charter to hold their forts and trading stations up to 1861 or 1862. We held some interesting arguments on the subject, and Williams, who was better posted than the doctor,, told him that their exclusive right was past and that in the near future all Oregon and the country up to the forty-ninth degree would be settled by Americans. Then, he said, they would have to move all their forts to the British side of the line. Dr. McLaughlin was somewhat surprised when Williams gave him the whole history of the country, and said he had not expected so much information from a trapper. All in all, we passed a very pleasant time with him, and he presented us with five gallons of port wine, inviting us to call again if we ever revisited this section.

We returned to Des Chutes River and camped about four miles above the Dog Indian village. They visited us daily, bringing fresh salmon. It was June and the fish were coming up the river.

In the meantime everything was being put in condition for fall trapping. George Howard remarked one day: "The people back in the States have no conception of the life of a trapper." One day it would be all peace and harmony, with the trappers enjoying life as few could even in civilization. The next day just the reverse, among hostile Indians.

CHAPTER XV

On September 16th we broke camp, knowing very little of our intended route, and not knowing whether the Indians we might meet would be friendly or hostile, but thoroughly prepared for every emergency.

We travelled over a rolling country, passing a warm spring where we saw a village. They were Warm Spring Indians, belonging, I think, to the Dog family. They did not appear very industrious, having poor lodges, very few ponies, and nothing to trade.

For several days we were busy trapping, and large quantities of beaver and otter were being caught. The country was beautiful. In every direction the scenery was grand and the region was a hunter's paradise for all kinds of game, particularly bear.

On Rush River we found the richest place for beaver we had yet come across, and it took us forty days to clean that section.

At one of our camps Howard made another of his characteristic remarks: "If people in the States could see this camp, with the immense number of beaver stretched on hoops and hanging on every available limb, they would go wild. When I return and tell them about it they will not believe me. Neither will they believe an account of the life of the trappers who appear to be perfectly at home in a country that none of them has ever heard of or seen."

It was now towards the last of October, and the weather looked stormy. We moved to a valley about ten miles from the Sierra Range of mountains, and by the time we had a corral built it was storming. By noon the next day there was over a foot of snow on the ground. Blacktail deer were seen in every direction, and we secured plenty of fresh meat.

We held a council and decided to cross the mountains before the snow got too deep.

From the summit of this range was the grandest view I ever beheld. To the westward lay a large valley, dotted with pine, alder, and cottonwood. Beyond, a large and beautiful lake sparkled in the sun as if dotted with diamonds. At this body of water, known afterwards as the Great Klamath Lake, was the scene of the Klamath and Modoc war in 1856, in which I was a participant.

We moved rapidly down the valley, sending six men in advance to select a winter camp. They chose a spot on a beautiful stream about a half mile from the lake.

Here we built our corral in the center of a grove of pine, and put up four lodges and three tents. We had an abundance of dry timber and pure water. Game and fish were on every side.

Since leaving the Warm Springs on Des Chutes River we had not come in contact with Indians, but an abundance of signs indicated that they were in close proximity.

On the third morning a party of fifteen appeared in camp, somewhat astonished at finding so large a body of whites. They saw at a glance that we were trappers. After they dismounted we invited them into our largest lodge, and feasted and smoked. They were well versed in sign-language, and Duranger could talk with them in Chinook. Lalick, their chief, asked all manner of questions. He was of medium size, dark complexioned, and with rather pleasant features. After our telling him that we intended to winter in this place, he was satisfied and assured us that we would not be molested by his people. Their village was about ten miles distant, on upper main Klamath River, and these Indians were on a hunt after elk, needing hides to repair their lodges. We unpacked some Indian goods and told them we would trade with them for any furs they might bring to camp. Martin were very plentiful in this section, and these Indians were adepts in taking them. A martin hide weighs about two ounces, and was worth in those days $6 per skin. The reason I mention this is to give some idea of the amount in value that could be packed on a horse. The average pack weighs one hundred and fifty pounds, which, if packed with martins, would mean in value $7200.

These Indians sometimes cross the Cascade Mountains to Willamette Valley to trade with the Hudson Bay Company. A few of the Hudson Bay trappers had passed through the country, but no such an outfit as ours. They knew that there was another class of white men called "Boston Men" (Americans). The Hudson Bay men were called "King George's Men," and are so called to-day when speaking to Indians in Chinook. East of the Rocky Mountains these Hudson Bay men were called "Redcoats" by the Indians.

Lalick told us that there was another tribe below this lake, on a smaller lake, and they were known as Cultus Siwash—bad Indians. These were the Modocs, whom we almost annihilated in 1856.

We passed the winter very profitably, many of the men learning the Chinook jargon, which was easily acquired. About every tribe of Indians west of the Rocky Mountains can converse in this language.

Here was the greatest contrast between two tribes, living in close proximity to each other. One was exceedingly friendly and very happy to have whites in their country. The other had a hatred against both whites and Indians. Up to this time neither tribe could have met with many whites.

We asked Lalick how many warriors the Cultus Siwash could muster, and he counted on his fingers several hundred.

We also found out that they had a few flintlock guns and many bows and arrows, the points of which were poisoned. Williams was always supplied with ammonia, which was considered an antidote for poison; it was used by scarifying the wound with the point of a knife and applying the ammonia, as well as freely inhaling its fumes.

That winter we enjoyed ourselves as few mountain men ever had, and before leaving this camp we invited to a final feast the head men of the village. Among these was the noted war chief, Comtucknay, a noble-looking Indian. After the feast we presented each one with some article, giving to Lalick and to Comtucknay each a Bannock pony.

Highly pleased with their entertainment, they shook hands and bade us farewell, and invited us to come again. Lalick advised us to keep along the base of the mountains to avoid meeting the Modocs. The advice was good, but was not heeded, as after results will show. The next morning we packed up and reached the lower end of the lake and remained there two days on account of rain. Beaver were scarce, and the time was spent in reading and looking after stock.

On the third day we started for Lost River, which empties into Tule Lake in the Modoc country, and explored it to its source, travelling through a beautiful valley, but found no beaver.

On our return trip down the valley we met a party of thirty Indians, who approached us at a rapid gait. They came up boldly and in an insulting manner ordered us to halt. They wanted to know what we were doing in their country. We told them our business and also produced pipes, saying, "We are friends."

They scornfully refused the proffered pipes, saying, "We do not smoke with white dogs." This was dangerous talk, for our men understood every word and could have made short work of them.

Their demand for horses was, of course, refused, and the manner in which they left indicated that trouble was ahead. These Indians talked Chinook and were good in sign-language.

We travelled east about six miles to a patch of timber, and were fortunate to find a good spring. A corral was built and rifle-pits dug, the men jokingly saying, "We are going to have another Bannock rupture with these devils." Just before sundown several Indians hovered around, taking in our situation, but did not come close enough to discover the preparations made for their reception.

Our war-horses were placed in the center of the corral, surrounded as much as possible by the pack-horses, so as to protect them from bullets and arrows. In the Bannock fight we had lost eleven pack-horses. On the north side of camp were some scattering pines, and should the Indians attack us in force this would be the danger point, although we had put up strong rifle-pits. These pits are constructed in the following manner. A long hole is dug to extend completely around the camp, the dirt being thrown up on the outside. On the top of the loose dirt we placed logs, making port-holes under the logs. When shooting through these holes the logs protected our heads. Our arms were, as usual, in prime condition. Rifles in those days were muzzle-loaders and so were pistols. Trappers were very expert in making cartridges for both arms and could load and shoot a rifle four times in a minute. I have seen some experts shoot five times a minute.

It was full moon, and this was greatly in our favor, as we did not know what tactics the Modocs would pursue.

Fifteen men were put on guard at a time, but nothing occurred in the night. At daylight we could see the Indians collecting on a high knoll about a mile and a half distant. Their every action was watched by Williams and others with spy-glasses.

All stock was watered and put back in corral, and we all ate breakfast. As these Indians used poisoned arrows the trappers prepared what they called their "coat of mail." All the men had heavy blacktail deer skins, which they wore over their shirts or coats, tied or buttoned up to the chin and reaching down to the thighs. Just prior to an engagement these were all soaked in water and wrung out. It is impossible for any arrow, whether iron or flint pointed, to penetrate buckskin so prepared. I have heard many people express doubts as to this, and I have always advised them to wet a piece of buckskin and try to penetrate it with a needle.

By eight o'clock fully two hundred Indians had assembled on the knoll and were holding a great council. I told Williams that I would give one hundred dollars to be there and hear their comments on the easy manner in which they were going to "capture these few white dogs" and all their horses. The thirty Indians whom we had met the day previous had counted our exact number, and had taken note of our fine horses and the many packs. All this would be magnified, whetting to a high degree the cupidity of the whole tribe.

CHAPTER XVI

The Modocs at length mounted, and in a leisurely manner approached to within three hundred yards of camp and halted. Two of their number dismounted and came towards camp holding up both hands, which was the sign for "we have no arms."

Williams and I met them, but we went thoroughly armed, as we noticed bows and arrows slung on their backs.

They were chiefs and asked us many insulting questions, calling us "dogs," demanding all our horses, guns, and, in fact, everything we had. In return for all this, they said that if we complied with their demands they would let us go. If we did not comply, they would rub us out, rubbing the palm of one hand over the other, signifying that they would annihilate us. Williams replied in a calm manner, and told them that they could have none of our goods. If they wished to smoke and make friends, good, and we would leave their country. I think, judging by their looks, that they thought we were afraid of them, for they told us to "go, dogs." Williams's eyes flashed fire, and I felt like making the Modocs eat their words. They stepped backwards for some distance, and we also.

The Indians now held a long council, after which about half of their number dismounted. Their intention was to rush camp and take it by assault. The footmen made a detour and reached the scattering pines. The horsemen divided, and we understood we would be attacked from all sides.

Fifteen men were detailed on the north side facing the scattered pines, with every preparation made for a hand-to-hand conflict. Each man had his tooth-pick or large knife in his belt, besides a trapping hatchet. The latter contained two pounds of steel, a sharp and dangerous weapon in the hands of determined men who were contending for their lives.

When the footmen reached the timber they gave a signal for the attack, which was responded to by the horsemen, who sent forth yell after yell, thinking, no doubt, it would paralyze us with fear, but it had the opposite effect. On the south and west the battle opened, and the war-whoops and yells sounded to us on the north as if pandemonium had broken loose.

The footmen began a charge, firing a few guns and sending a flight of arrows. We reserved our fire until they had come within forty yards of the rifle-pits. The Modocs could not see us and, having noticed that no shots came from that side, they must have thought that we were all contending against the horsemen, for they came on a run and in close body.

We emptied our rifles and completely surprised them, for they halted and looked bewildered. Then the shotguns and Colts were brought into play with terrible effect, almost every shot bringing down an Indian.

Seventeen of their bravest warriors made a charge to the east of us and almost reached the corral, when ten of our party met them at close quarters. It was a furious hand-to-hand conflict and showed the great superiority of palefaces over Indians. Pistols, knives and hatchets did terrible work, and in less time than it takes to tell it fifteen of the Indians were dead, two of the attacking party making their escape. There were no casualties among the trappers, except a few scratches.

While the hand-to-hand fight was going on, the five men in the rifle-pits kept the rest of the Indians at bay. The ground in front of our breastwork was literally covered with sprawling Indians, many of whom crawled to the trees and were helped away by their comrades.

After this repulse it was simply a tree fight on our side.

On the south side of the camp a hot fight was raging, and some of us rushed over just in time to assist in repelling a furious charge. Three of our men were down and several others wounded, but the latter were not disabled. On this charge the Modocs came up to within fifty feet of the rifle-pits, but with all their bravery they could not withstand the steady fire of the trappers, and they soon withdrew to a safe distance.

Many women arrived and rendered assistance, taking the dead and wounded back to their village amid the most dismal howls that I have ever heard.

At a signal from the chief, the Indians collected in a body to hold council.

We had lost three good and brave men who had been in many a desperate engagement. These we buried while the Indians were holding council.

A single Indian was soon seen approaching and he was met by Williams and myself, and we asked him what he wanted. He said he wanted us to stop fighting and to let them take off the dead and wounded. We told him to send for the women and pack them off. He returned to the main body, and in a short time the women appeared leading ponies. They packed two bodies on a pony, and acted as if they were frightened to death, not knowing what manner of men we were. We dragged out the fifteen who had been killed in the hand-to-hand struggle, and they soon had them all packed off.

Many of our men were in favor of making a charge, knowing that we could rout them with ease. Ours was certainly the first large party that they had come in contact with. They had, no doubt, met with smaller outfits, for we found on them several trappers' knives. At all events, they knew our exact numbers and they made sure of having overwhelming odds in their favor, expecting to win easily. Where their calculations failed was in their ignorance of the trappers' arms. They did not know that each one was armed with two six-shooters, and that we had seven double-barreled shotguns besides the rifles. Had they known these things I doubt very much if they would have attacked us in the manner in which they did.

After collecting all their dead and wounded the Indians withdrew.

An incident occurred in this same grove during the Modoc war of 1856, which will well illustrate the difference between the whites and Indians in attack and defense.

General Crosby was commander of the whites, and in his command was a company of sixty rangers, the original California Rangers of which I was a member. The Modocs were in possession of this grove, with the rangers on the outside, just the reverse of our present fight. The Indians outnumbered the rangers two to one, but in just one half hour's fighting the rangers routed the Indians, inflicting considerable loss, and secured possession of the grove.

After the Indians had retired, we turned out our horses to graze, protected by a guard of ten men, mounted on their war-horses.

Some of the men climbed to the tops of high knolls, so as to get the lay of the land. As yet we had collected no furs this spring, and as there was no possibility of a trade with the Modocs, we determined to break camp the next day, Indians permitting.

Our intention was to travel eastward to the base of the Sierra Nevada. During the day we strengthened our position somewhat to prepare for another defense, as Lalick had claimed that the Modocs numbered several hundred.

Stock was left out until dark, and all kept a sharp lookout. A few scattering Indians could be seen towards the lake, but none seemed inclined to make our acquaintance. The Indians must have called together all their medicine men to explain the cause of the disastrous defeat at the hands of a few "white dogs." At all events they did not bother us during the night.

At daybreak all our belongings were packed and, mounting our war-horses, we started. Ten men acted as an advance guard. Ten brought up the rear, and five on each flank. At every point we were prepared to repel an attack. We proceeded south for about three miles and struck a lodge pole trail leading from the lake, going east. We followed this trail to the foot of a bluff having a rise of some three hundred feet.

It was on top of this bluff that the massacre of twenty-nine emigrants by the Modocs occurred in 1852. Only three men made their escape to Yreka, Cal., and reported the occurrence.

Ben Wright, an old mountain man, collected a company of his acquaintances to avenge this slaughter of men, women, and children. He met the Modocs on Lost River at Natural Rocky Ford, about twelve miles from our battle ground, and after a hand-to-hand conflict routed the Indians with considerable loss. That was the second defeat for the Modocs.

Emigrants taking the Saunders cut-off to northern California and southern Oregon used to pass over this trail, but after the massacre they travelled by other routes. The place where the massacre occurred is called to-day "Bloody Point."

CHAPTER XVII

We travelled east for about ten miles and reached Clear Lake, a beautiful body of water. Plenty of Indian signs were in evidence, but no Indians.

For camp we selected a small point of land which extended out into the lake, and dug a few rifle-pits. Deer and antelope were plenty and we secured quantities of fresh meat. By this time we had come to the conclusion that the Modocs were not as numerous as Lalick had reported, or they surely would have given us another battle.

Next day we continued east to a fair-sized stream running south, a branch of the noted Pitt River, but not known to us at that time.

In July, 1844, we reached a beautiful valley called to-day Honey Lake Valley, but at that time without a name. We remained here three months, enjoying ourselves as only men can who love the grandeur of nature. Our time was spent in exploring, hunting, fishing, reading, and practicing with all arms.

Many Indians came to camp bringing furs, for which we traded. They appeared to be very poor and were very indifferent sign-talkers, although we got along with them for a time. Towards the last they commenced stealing, and when caught doing this we let them feel the weight of whips applied by "Kentucky George," who understood his business. At this the Indians ceased their visits, which was a sign to look out for some devilment. We always kept guard both night and day. By experienced mountain men that practice is never omitted.

Early one morning shots were fired by the guards, and we rushed out just as an Indian ran by the lodge. One shot put an end to him. The guards had killed four others with shotguns. As it was break of day we scouted the valley for some distance, but discovered no more Indians.

We had treated these Indians with all kindness, and their acts in trying to steal offended the men. Some were in favor of attacking the village.

We held a council and determined to set an example by cremating the five whom we had killed.

This was done in an "approved manner," as Perkins said. There was plenty of pitch pine and other dry material close at hand, and the dead Indians were carefully placed in the center of a big pile. By noon only ashes were left, which brought forth Perkins's remark.

I have been told by intelligent men that it was cruel in us to cremate these Indians. Wherein the cruelty? Do not our leading scientists advocate cremation as the proper mode of disposing of the dead? It was practiced in both ancient and modern times. Bear in mind that ninety-eight per cent, of mountain men were pronounced free-thinkers, and as a rule they were more humane, more generous, truer to friends, with less deception than those in civilization, with few exceptions.

We held several councils as to our future route. Some who had been in southern California advocated returning by way of Los Angeles. Others wanted to take the eastern route by way of Carson City. This route was finally decided on, as the prospect for collecting furs was better; and about the 10th of October we broke camp and moved in a southerly direction along the base of the mountains.

On leaving camp we noticed a few Indians watching our movements, no doubt glad of our departure, as they would be able to recover their five friends. They probably found the ashes. It would be a lesson for them to leave white men's horses alone, and it would be commented on for many a moon in their councils.

We trapped all the streams leading from the mountains, and reached Pyramid Lake in what is now the State of Nevada. Here we met a village of Pah Utes, who were able to converse in the Shoshone language. I noticed that a few of them had flint and steel such as trappers used for making fire, but the majority used sticks.

They thought we were a new tribe of white men because we used pads on our runners and were bronzed like Indians. Here we traded for a few furs, but we offended the Indians when we refused to let them have our best horses.

Our next stop was on the Truckee River, and during the journey we saw more blacktail deer than I have ever seen before or since. It was a hunter's paradise, with the streams full of fish and blue grouse in every direction. A blue grouse is the daintiest of food and has no equal among fowl.

At the upper end of this river is a large lake and beautiful valley, which in 1853 were called Biglow's Lake and Valley, but later on, I am told, were renamed Strawberry Lake and Valley. In 1844 the lake had no name, the Indians in signs calling it "Upper Lake."

A small band of Indians had their village about a half mile from our camp. They were a miserable and degraded set. I doubt if our ancestors of a million years back could have been more so. They could properly be classed with the savages of the flint age, as they used flint for the points of arrows and spears, of indifferent manufacture. Game was readily approached and they were easily able to supply themselves with meat, while they were expert in catching fish. They were notorious beggars and thieves.

As we left this camp dark clouds began to gather, foreboding heavy snow, and we started to cross the mountains. At noon it began to snow, and when on the summit the trail was completely obliterated. Any but experienced mountain men would have been bewildered, and as it was it put us all on our mettle. Imagine yourselves driving two hundred and fifty horses, and with the snowflakes falling so fast and thick that all view was obliterated, and you will have some idea of our condition. To extricate ourselves without the loss of some of the livestock in this strange country, among dense forests of pine, cool and practical judgment was required. In such an instance there must be no bewilderment or everything is lost. I observed in the features of all the men a coolness and determination which would have been commendable in any general in a desperate battle, where victory or defeat hung in the balance. Ten men rode in advance, two abreast; all loose stock following. The remainder of the trappers rode on each side of the loose stock to keep them from straggling.

We followed a given course, taking the light breeze for a guide. Soon we found ourselves going down a steep ridge, floundering through deep snow, not knowing where we should bring up, and finally reached a plateau.

We could not see any distance, but as it would not do to camp here, we journeyed on, keeping to the right, as we thought, and hurrying along, for it was getting late. The old saying is "fortune favors the brave." In this case it favored us.

For half an hour we continued our course, descending all the time, and at length came to a level bottom. To our left we heard a fall of water, and found there a small creek fringed with cottonwood. We soon had our lodges and tents up and all packs secure in a large tent. The horses were turned out to graze with six men as guards. The snow was now fully twelve inches deep. Here our spades came well into play; while some shoveled snow, others collected a quantity of dry wood, and none too soon, for when the last load of wood was brought in it was dark. There was no time to build a corral, so the horses were tied to trees. The snow was still falling, and it looked gloomy.

We did not know what kind of a country we were in. All we were certain of was water and timber on our left and the level we were camped on. Whether there were any Indians in the neighborhood we had no time to ascertain, but we kept a guard—two men at a time—with one hour reliefs. I have been in many a dismal place, but none more so than this. Several of the men had watches, and when daylight should have appeared it was still dark and the snow was still falling. At seven o'clock the snow was two feet deep, with no sign of abating. We untied the horses and sent a strong guard with them in case of a stampede, although a hundred of them had chains on their fore-fetlocks.

It stopped snowing at two o'clock, but continued cloudy. The next morning the sun made its appearance. A white shroud covered the country as far as the eye could see, but on one point we were satisfied, and that was that we were out of the mountains. We remained in this camp four days, by which time most of the snow had disappeared. On the morning of the fifth day we moved along the base of the mountains, crossing several high ridges, until we came to a small valley and creek. From a high promontory we had a fair view of the surrounding country. To the south was an open low-lying valley, which some of our men pronounced Carson Valley, and declared that the shining looking country beyond was the Great American Desert.

Our next camp was on Carson River, and we selected a strong position, as Indian signs were abundant. A sight which gave us much encouragement was the many beaver signs.

We had just finished putting up our tents and lodges when a dozen mounted Indians rode into camp. They were Pah Utes and very intelligent, and told us their village was some distance below our camp. They asked us where we had come from, and seemed pleased when we told them that we intended remaining all winter to trap the streams. They next asked us to give them some of the beaver meat which they relished highly. All the beaver they secured was what they shot with arrows. A few of these Indians understood a little Spanish, which showed that they had come in contact with that people. Besides, they had a few Spanish flintlock guns, but no ammunition. They had to depend for meat wholly on bows and arrows. Antelope were plentiful, but notwithstanding their expertness in the use of bows, they often suffered from lack of food. They caught a great many fish, such as suckers and whitefish, but these are poor eating.

We invited the Indians to sup with us, and the quantity of food they devoured would have astonished a gourmand from the East. I suppose it was the first square meal they had partaken of for years. After supper the Indians departed, notifying us that they would see us the next day.

That night we set traps and put only one man on guard. Our sleep was undisturbed—a rare thing in a trapper's life.

The next morning at daylight the stock was turned out with two herders, and all the others went after beaver, returning with a good catch. After breakfast the skinners went at the beaver, and had the hides off when the Indians made their appearance. They were astonished at the number of beaver we had caught. When we told the women they could take the skinned beaver with them, they were pleased beyond expression, and insisted on shaking every one of us by the hand.

For the next six weeks we were busy handling furs, and experienced no difficulty with these Indians. Peace and harmony prevailed, and the general routine of a trapper's life was unbroken.

On the 25th of February, 1845, we parted from our Indian friends, the whole village having assembled to see us off, and all united in cordially inviting us to come again to their country.

From the camp on Carson River we took the Indian trail to what is now called Humboldt Lake, fifty miles across the desert, reaching there at five o'clock with all our horses in prime condition.

We trapped up the river to a rocky point, when a war-party of fifty Indians intercepted us and wanted to know what we were doing in their country. In an arrogant manner they demanded some of our horses and many other things. These Indians were a branch of the Pah Utes, and we plainly saw that unless we were very careful we should have trouble with them. With all Williams's diplomatic tricks he could not induce them to smoke the pipe of peace, and they departed looking daggers at us. As there were plenty of beaver signs we determined to trap here, even if we had to fight. We constructed corrals and prepared for every emergency.

That night we set our traps and were not disturbed, but we suspected that the Indians were up to some deviltry.

Next morning the trappers all returned, with the exception of Frederick Crawford, who had set traps some distance from camp. As he failed to return at ten o'clock, ten of us mounted and went to see what had become of him.

Docket, who was next outside trapper, had seen Crawford setting traps at a bend in the river at some distance, and to that point we went.

Scouting to some Cottonwood groves to make sure there was no ambush, we went in and soon discovered where traps had been set and also Indian tracks. Then we were satisfied that Crawford had gone under. We saw where his horse had stood and, going to a thick bunch of willows, we found the ground saturated with blood. The Indians had lain hidden in this bunch of willows, knowing that the trapper would come in the morning to look after his traps. By the signs the Indians had made there must have been six or eight of them. They had thrown Crawford in the river, which was four feet deep. We could easily see him and soon had him out.

When we had poor Crawford out on the bank, I would have liked to have present one of those sensitive beings who hold up their hands in horror when they hear of a trapper scalping an Indian.

He was scalped, his eyes were gouged out, his face was slashed with a knife, and he was otherwise mutilated in a way too horrible to describe.

Crawford, who came from Texas, was a handsome man, six feet tall, well educated, brave, kind, and generous. We found five of Crawford's traps and four beaver. The Indians got the remainder, with his rifle, two pistols, and a horse.

We were soon back in camp with the body of our comrade. When our men saw Crawford it was plain that death would be the penalty to any of those Indians should they be caught.

We dug a secret grave and, wrapping Crawford up in his blankets, put him carefully away. No monument marks the grave where this kind and brave man was laid to rest. Such too often was the fate of trappers, many of them not even receiving burial.

At two in the afternoon our pickets signaled, "Indians coming on horseback." We soon had all our stock in corral and were prepared at every point. The pickets now came in and reported having counted sixty Indians. They soon made their appearance on a ridge, about three hundred yards from camp. They delivered one shot, which came so close that some of the trappers said, "That is Crawford's rifle; we will recapture it."

The Indians now challenged us to come out and fight. Crawford's death had cut our number down to thirty-eight, but that did not matter. It was impossible to hold the men in. Leaving three men to take care of camp, the others mounted and started out.

When the Indians saw us mount they gave yell after yell, thinking, no doubt, that we would become paralyzed with fear. They divided and charged us from two sides. We let them get to within one hundred yards, when we halted and brought our rifles into play. Dropping rifles on the ground, we charged them pistols in hand. Fully twenty-five Indians fell from the rifle shots. This bewildered them, and before they could recover we were amongst them.

A fight like this lasts only a few minutes, and very few Indians made their escape. One tall Indian was riding Crawford's horse and he tried to get away, but delayed too long. One of our men caught him and recovered horse, rifle, and pistols.

We captured forty-three ponies and collected all such plunder as we cared for, besides ridding the earth of a lot of insulting Indians. Crawford was fully avenged.

A few of our men received arrow wounds, but none were serious. We lost but two horses, shot in the breast.

This was undoubtedly the first fight these Indians had made against an outfit like ours, otherwise they would have exercised better generalship. The main secret of the trappers' success was in making every shot count in the first volley. This bewildered the Indians, and before they could collect their thoughts we rushed in among them.

There was no question that our outfit was the most effective fighting body of trappers on the plains. It contained men who, I firmly believe, would have been able to command an army. It is a question in my mind if any soldiers of any nation were as well drilled in the use of rifles and pistols as this body of trappers.

The horses also were drilled to stand fire and to be quick in evolutions. The war-whoops and yells of Indians did not affect them. They simply pricked up their ears or looked unconcerned.

After the fight we held a council and decided that it would be best to move from this place, as we did not know how many warriors these Indians could muster. At any rate, it would not be safe for one or two men to go any distance from camp after furs.

We now raised all our traps and by three o'clock started up the river. A few Indians could be seen riding swiftly along the base of the mountains, for what purpose we could not tell, nor did we care. We were aware of one thing, and that was that they would be anxious to find out about those Indians who failed to return to the village. The reader may be certain that when they found that their invincible warriors had gone to their happy hunting grounds without their scalp-locks, there would be much wailing, gashing of flesh, and cutting off of fingers.

They would be occupied for some time to come with the laying away of their braves, and also in calling on all their medicine-men for an explanation. Poor Crawford's scalp at this time would suffer untold indignities.

CHAPTER XVIII

We reached what is called Thousand Spring Valley after dark and unpacked, but kept all stock close. We built no fires and put up no lodges.

By daylight we had packed and at two o'clock we reached Raft River. A short distance below smoke was discernible, which on investigation proved to be from a camp of seven Hudson Bay men, who were trapping.

We soon had a feast prepared and invited these men to join us, for they looked hungry and crestfallen. Duranger, who was acquainted with them, asked the cause, and they replied that the Indians had stolen seven head of horses from them, leaving three, a number insufficient to pack their furs.

These big companies treated their men like peons. They were poorly armed, and had but a scant supply of food. They had to depend on their own resources and live on what the country produced, which to them meant beaver meat and berries in season. The story of the Hudson Bay Company's treatment of their employees is too well known to be commented on, although I will say that if I had my choice between being a slave with some masters in Missouri or being a Hudson Bay employee, I would prefer the former. We gave each one of them an Indian pony, giving them a bill of sale, so that they could show their title to the "busware" (bourgeois = boss). We also traded seven more of the Indian ponies for furs, and advised them to leave this section, as the Indians would most likely follow us. And what chance would these men have, armed with a few old Hudson Bay flint-lock guns? They took our advice and accompanied us to Goose Creek, west of the Goose Mountains. Here we separated, the Canadians going down Goose Creek and we continuing on to Bear River.

We trapped Bear River and crossed over to Green River, picking up considerable fur. We then crossed over to Warm Land via the Big Wind River Valley and visited the hot springs, remaining there three days.

We met four trappers coming from the lower country, where they had lost all their horses and one companion, killed by Blackfeet. These men were strangers to all of us and stated that they were employed by the Northwestern Fur Company. We presented each one of these with a pony and advised them to get out of this section, as Blackfeet war-parties were numerous. They took our advice, but they did not seem aware of the danger. It was a sin for these companies to send out a few men, poorly armed, on these trapping expeditions. They cared nothing for the lives of their employees. All they wanted was furs.

We held a general council as to what route we should take, as the trapping season was over. Many of the men had decided to take a trip East to visit relations. All of them, except Duranger and "Scotty," came from three States, Missouri, Kentucky, and Virginia. We finally decided to cut across country and go to the North Platte River to pick up a few buffalo. We arrived at the mouth of the Laramie River without mishap, and there met an emigrant train going to Oregon. This occurrence brought home the truth of Williams's prediction to Dr. McLaughlin. It was also our first intimation of the Mormon migration to Salt Lake Valley.

Twenty-five of our men concluded to go to St. Louis and take their furs with them. Our party or mess sold our furs to buyers who were present, and settled up everything among ourselves. The original thirteen all returned.

Thus more than a band of brothers parted company, few of them to meet again. Many remained in the East and settled down. Williams went to Santa Fe, accompanied by Perkins and six others. It was the only sad parting I have ever experienced.

An exploring party desired to visit the Big Horn Mountains, and engaged Docket, Noble, Evans, Russell and myself to accompany them. This party was sent out by the Northwestern Fur Company, as we afterwards found out, to ascertain if there were a favorable location to establish a trading-post in that section. Had we been aware of this we would not have gone, although they paid us well.

On Powder River we had to take to timber in order to stand off a war-party of thirty Blackfeet. There were ten in our party, but only five armed as prairie men should be in those days. The Indians shot several times at long range, and we emptied three of their saddles, and to our disgust were blamed by our employer. None of his party had ever been in a battle, and they knew very little about Indians. The head of the party was named Overstall, and he was an arrogant sort of a fellow, who thought we were like the remainder of the Northwestern Fur Company's employees. We took pleasure in informing him that we belonged to the free traders and trappers, and held all the big companies in contempt. We also told him to let up with his arrogance or we would leave him and let him get out of the country as best he could.

An imbecile proposition that he made was for us to go and have a talk with the Indians, and let them know we were their friends. The idea of meeting Blackfeet Indians, after having been run into the timber and shot at, was preposterous—not to be thought of for a moment.

It was about ten o'clock in the morning when the Indians forced us to take to timber, and they hovered around until three, occasionally throwing a shot at us at long range. We wasted no more ammunition, though had they come within range it would have been different.

The old man thought that this point would make a very desirable location for a trading post. We were within one mile of where Fort Reno was established years afterwards.

Finally the Indians disappeared, and Docket, Noble and myself mounted our horses and scouted the country for two miles, taking the Indian trail, which led towards the south end of the Big Horn Mountains. On our return we reported that these Indians were either Blood or Piegans, as those two branches of the Blackfeet often went to war mounted.

The old man just then remembered that he had pressing and important business on Platte River and at St. Louis, and that there was not a moment to spare in getting there. He and his four companions had an attack of the ague. They asked if we could find our way back in the night? If so, they would make it worth our while to reach Laramie River as soon as possible. It was disgusting to see such cowardice. We ate, mounted, and started, and travelled at a lively gait. They asked us many times if we thought the Indians would follow us. To these questions we answered " No, but we might come across others," which was true, although we did not expect to.

About midnight we halted and made coffee and lunched. We told the old man to eat and then sleep for two or three hours, for he appeared exhausted. His men spread blankets for him and he lay down, but not to sleep, for every few minutes he would rise and ask if there were any danger yet. We told him to sleep, that we would look out for him.

After two hours he could stand it no longer, and begged us to saddle up as soon as possible, as he had a premonition that the Indians were upon us. His thoughts dwelt on nothing but Indians.

We started and reached Rush Creek on North Platte River, opposite where Fort Fetterman now stands, at seven in the morning. Some Mormons were camped there. The old man and his men were completely worn out. There was not much force or snap in any of them. We cooked breakfast and called the old man, but he could not eat, though he emptied a flask of brandy, with which he was well supplied. He invited us to partake of it, but we declined with thanks, saying that he would require all he had for himself and friends. We remained there overnight, the old man evidently forgetting that his presence was urgently needed in St. Louis.

We reached Laramie on the second day, depositing Overstall and his four men at Tebeau's, all five of them being in a condition fit for the hospital.

Overstall settled with us and said he would get his company to give us employment. We thanked him and told him his company had not sufficient means to employ us, and then added that we were free trappers and would not be employed by any one.

Docket, Noble, Evans, Russell, and myself remained together for many years, and were known as the "Tartar outfit."

CHAPTER XIX

We had a few things stored at Green River, so we returned there and settled up.

Washakie was preparing to start on his fall hunt in the Big Horn country and we mentioned to him that we would like to accompany the village. Besides wishing to explore that section, we were desirous of studying more accurately the habits and characteristics of the Shoshones. Washakie was delighted, and we bought one thousand dollars' worth of choice Indian goods to trade, as the opportunity might occur.

We started on the first day of October, travelling by easy stages. At night the young folks would keep the village awake until midnight with their singing and dancing. They enjoyed life for all it was worth, giving no heed to the morrow. A happy aggregation on the whole, one to be envied by many. The older members of the camp would hold councils and would speculate on what tribes were most likely to be met with on the journey.

In eight days we crossed the Snake Range of mountains and found our first buffalo, a small herd of about two hundred. About seventy-five Indians mounted their best horses and started after them. It was a sight worth going hundreds of miles to see, and only the pen of Mark Twain could describe the ridiculous mishaps which occurred,—ponies falling, riders going heels overhead, getting up with a yell, remounting, and off again in pursuit of some wounded buffalo.

They secured over two hundred head, which was an abundance, although large quantities of meat were required to supply a village of one hundred lodges.

We crossed the Big Horn River and proceeded to the noted Stinking Water. Washakie pointed out the hot springs, and on the west side of the main Stinking Water we saw several sulphur springs which were apparently dying out. The main spring is in the canon at the base of the mountain, and its fumes can be smelled for miles. I have heard it said that there were sulphur springs on the north and south forks of Stinking Water; but we did not see them, nor did Washakie mention the fact.

We had been in this camp seven days when a party of Crow Indians arrived on a visit to the Shoshones. They said their village was on another river called Sun Dance (Clark's Fork), and that they had come over to see their friends. They brought three good-looking ponies and wanted to race.

The Crows are not as intelligent as the Shoshones, and are not to be compared with them in independence and cleanliness. They are noted beggars and pilferers, and it is the reverse with Shoshones. You can, with perfect safety, trust them with everything you possess. I was not much acquainted with the Crows at this time, having met them only once before on the Sweetwater River, and then only a war-party.

On the second day the racing commenced, and the Shoshones ran their second-class ponies so as to let the Crows win. The Crows went wild and thought they had invincible ponies.

In the afternoon the Shoshones brought out their race-horses, and they were an indifferent looking outfit. The Crows were positive that they had a sure thing and they bet everything they had, and on being bantered by the Shoshones to bet their race-horses, jumped at the opportunity.

It was a sure thing on the Shoshones' side, for in the previous races they had gauged the speed of the Crow ponies.

The distance was one mile over prairie. They do not prepare a smooth track. Such an idea never enters the Indian mind. Young Indian boys, stripped naked, are mounted on the ponies and led to the starting point. There is no jockeying such as white men indulge in, and no foolishness either. The order is given to go, and the first horse passing the winning post wins the race. It makes no difference what becomes of the other horses. Falling down or flying the track cuts no figure. This system is the same amongst all Indians, and the same rule applies in foot-racing. Ninety-nine times out of a hundred the best horse wins in an Indian race.

After the races the Crows departed, crestfallen, but promising to come again and bring other horses.

It was now a busy time with the Indians, who were hard at work curing meat and making pemmican. We were also busy and caught many beaver, otter, mink, and martin, and killed six fine black bears. Buffalo were more plentiful than usual and Washakie told us that the medicine-men gave us the credit for their abundance.

We had only one difficulty with war-parties, and that of minor importance. A few Blackfeet stole some of our ponies and drove them into the mountains. A small party started after them one morning, and by three o'clock were back in the village with the ponies and one scalp.

In the latter part of November, the Indians having all the meat and robes they required, we started on our return trip to Green River.

On the 15th of December we reached Green River and sold all our furs to traders. We set up our lodge next to Washakie's, and had many interesting conversations with him. He had heard of our fight at Rocky Point with the Pah Utes, and gave us credit for having inflicted the punishment they merited, for they were bad Indians. He thought that they would not soon forget this lesson.

We asked Washakie if these Humboldts or Pah Utes were not Shoshone Indians, and he answered that they were, but that they did not recognize them or any of the Pah Utes or Utahs, though they met sometimes and traded.

We also asked Washakie if the Shoshone had occupied and claimed this section of the country, and his answer was that they claimed the country to the Elk River (Yellowstone), and had done so as far back as they and their fathers could recollect. He said the Crows, Flatheads, and Nez Perces hunted upon their land. In fact, it was held by other tribes as neutral ground, claiming the right to hunt thereon.

I asked the chief if he had any idea whence sign-language originated, and he answered as many other old Indians have, that he did not know. It was handed down from father to son. Don Alvares, a Chilean, once told me that the Indians who occupied the base of the Andes Mountains used almost the same signs as the North American Indians.

After disposing of our furs we went south to the Arkansas. The next two years and a half of my life had no bearing on prairie life, and I will pass it over. In 1846 the Mexican War commenced, and almost all the trappers joined General Price's forces.

In the spring of 1848 I returned to St. Louis promising to meet my four companions at Green River in the fall.

I went home and remained there six weeks. Everything had changed. Many of my schoolmates had married and settled down or departed to new pastures. My people were anxious for me to remain and settle down, but after tasting the free life of the prairie it was now too late. Both of my parents passed away within a year afterwards and our family scattered to the four winds, many of them never to meet again. " Westward, Ho!" appeared to take possession of every one. Rumor spread that gold had been discovered in California, which by the treaty with Mexico now belonged to the United States. Emigrants were moving to Oregon by the hundreds. Salt Lake was being rapidly settled by the Mormons, and the whole country was assuming a new aspect. By the whole country I mean California, Oregon, and Salt Lake.

On the 25th of July I took steamboat for Council Bluffs and visited old Sarpee, who had a trading-post at a place called Plattsburg. The old man was anxious to have me remain and do the trading with the Indians who frequently visited there.

An Oregon emigrant train came to the post, intending to travel on the north side of the Platte River, crossing the Missouri at Kanesville, which was a new Mormon town. The captain wanted to get an experienced man to pilot the train, and I offered to take it as far as Green River and find him some one there to take it over the remainder of the trip. After consulting with his outfit he offered me $250 and a fine five-year-old horse, which I accepted.

The train consisted of twenty-five wagons drawn by mules and oxen, and the people had with them a number of milch cows. In the party were fifteen women and several children. They came chiefly from Kentucky and Indiana. The captain's name was Reeves. He was a fine gentleman of about fifty years of age.

We crossed the ferry without mishap and moved steadily along until we reached the left fork of Platte River, where we came in contact with a party of Pawnee Indians.

They wanted to trade their ponies for some of the blooded Kentucky horses in our train, and were angry when we refused, saying that the Sioux would steal them all.

They would have made a dash for the horses right then if I had not placed well-armed guards around them.

We made a corral of the wagons, fastening them together with chains, and at night placed the stock inside.

Four men went on guard at a time, the captain and I going on at two A.m. We had not been on guard an hour when I heard the hooting of an owl. I told the captain to get more men out quietly.

The hooting ceased, and when the Indians had crawled close to the corral they gave their war whoop, thinking they could stampede the stock. These were tied by halters to the inside wagon wheels, and although the yells did create, some disturbance among the stock, none got away.

After the first yell they made a rush for the corral with furious war-whoops, expecting to paralyze these strangers. They were met by a murderous fire. Ten men had been placed in front of the tents with orders to lie low. About six Indians made a dash for the tents and were met by a volley from the shotguns, which killed four of them. The Indians now disappeared, leaving nine of their number on the field. I told the captain that it was customary for mountain men to scalp Indians. He laughed and advised me to let it go, as it might shock the ladies. These ladies showed remarkable presence of mind and nerve. They had rolled up their bedding, placing it on the outside so as to form a breastwork, and had lain down behind it with the children.

At daylight we pulled out and travelled about fifteen miles and camped on a bend of the river, making a corral of the wagons. The ladies asked me if I thought the Indians would try to revenge themselves on us, and I answered that as they were unsuccessful in getting our outfit, they might decide to leave us alone and try to get even on some other train. This very often happened and the fault lay with emigrants themselves who did not take proper precautions. All emigrants had been warned time and time again to be very careful, but they seemed indifferent to their surroundings and neglected taking precaution. The result was that their stock was run off, leaving them helpless on the prairie with their families and wagons. Soldiers had to come to their assistance.

The Pawnees did not follow us nor did we see anything more of them.

We passed many small parties of Mormons, who appeared poor and miserable. Some of them were afoot and were pulling or pushing small hand-carts.

We saw no more Indians until we reached Ash Hollow, which was on the opposite side of the river. This is a noted place, where General Harney had a fight with the Sioux. About seventy-five Cheyennes visited the camp, many of whom I was acquainted with, but had not met them since 1842, when trading on Cherry Creek. They asked me many questions: Where had I been? Where was I going? Who were these people?

The ladies prepared a feast and invited the Indians, who were led by White Antelope, a noted chief and a proud and fine-looking warrior. They behaved remarkably well for Indians, not begging and only once offering to trade horses.

We moved steadily along, day after day, without obstruction or annoyance of any kind. Antelope and grouse were plentiful, and there was always an abundance of fresh meat in camp.

We reached Fort Hall October first, and I parted from one of the most accomplished emigrant outfits that ever crossed the plains.

I remained at Fort Hall for three days at the request of Captain H. Grant, who was employed by the Hudson Bay Company. He was a tall Highland Scotchman, and had been in the employ of the company for thirty years, and his reminiscences of the great Mackenzie and Frazer rivers would fill volumes of most interesting matter.

One thing struck me forcibly, and that was the manner in which his company recruited their forces. Every year their agents in Scotland would get recruits from the Shetland and Orkney Islands, who would sign agreements to serve the company for from three to five years at twenty-five pounds a year and to live on what the country produced.

On their arrival in Canada the men were induced to take upon themselves a wife, an Indian woman. Calico in those days was fifty cents a yard, other things in proportion, and at the end of their term of service they were overwhelmingly in debt to the company. They were then kept in service to work out this indebtedness. Mexican peons and Hudson Bay employees were in much the same condition.

The Northwestern Fur Company differed very little from the Hudson Bay Company in the treatment of its employees. These companies did not like to be interfered with in collecting furs and robes from the Indians, and endeavored to have a law passed making it a felony for any except themselves to do this trading; also to compel all trappers to be in their employ.

Mountain men had more influence with the Indians than they, and they were aware of it, and from this sprang the feeling of antagonism which I retain to this day.

CHAPTER XX

On the road to Fort Bridger I passed two trains bound for Oregon, which contained many women and children, and one Mormon outfit.

There were several Mormons at the Fort and a visible change had taken place. We were all aware that in a very few years a great emigration would take place, but we had not looked for the Mormons migrating to Salt Lake.

In every direction rumors were afloat of large gold discoveries in California, and all the trappers were discussing the possibility of making fortunes.

Two days before I reached Bridger a war party of Indians had run off thirty horses belonging to the men at the Fort, who followed them for a day without success. They were a poor lot of men, who eked out an existence by just hanging around trading-posts. We trappers called them "doby men."

I continued on to Brown's Hole rendezvous and found there my four partners, as well as fifteen of our old companions.

The next day a couple of wagons arrived from Weston, Missouri, laden with goods for trading purposes. They brought news of great excitement throughout the East over the California gold discoveries; and that a great many people were taking ship, some going around Cape Horn and others by the Panama route. The news created much excitement at the rendezvous, as the majority had not heard of it before. A council was held by the trappers on the advisability of starting at once for California, taking the southern trail. Our party decided to wait until spring and take the Humboldt trail, striking middle California. We believed that if any gold were there, it would probably be in that section of the country.

Among the arrivals were three gentlemen, two from St. Louis and one from Kentucky, who were anxious to have a hunt in the Big Horn Mountains. They had heard and read a great deal about that romantic country, and of the wild and free life of the American trapper and mountaineer, and they were desirous of investigating in person with a view of publishing an account of their trip.

We warned them that it was a dangerous country at all seasons of the year, but that ten trappers would see them through. They were eager to go and offered to engage ten trappers for two months, furnish the outfit, and pay each trapper $100 a month. Besides this, the trappers could take their traps and retain all furs caught, as they were anxious to see in what manner beaver and otter were caught.

While these gentlemen were making their offer, Perkins arrived from Las Vegas, bringing a letter to me from Williams, who wanted me to come there and go into partnership with him in trading. I should certainly have gone had I not decided on the California trip. I never saw Williams again. A few years afterwards the Southern Utes killed him by mistake in Apache Pass. They were, great friends of old Bill, and they packed him to their village and gave him a chief's burial, mourning for him as for one of their own. The Utes themselves told me this.

Perkins and I accepted the offer of these eastern men and made up a party of ten trappers. There were several Indians at the rendezvous who had ponies for trade, and our outfit was soon furnished. The trip was a most enjoyable one for all concerned, game of every description was abundant, and the easterners became good hunters. They were highly pleased at their success and paid each man double what they had agreed to.

The Shoshones discovered our camp on Nine Blackfeet Sleep Creek, so called because nine Blackfeet Indians were caught asleep by the Shoshones, who forced them to continue their sleep indefinitely.

The day the Shoshones found us, "Silver Tip" was on duty as picket. He could almost scent an Indian a mile off, and his eyes were as keen and penetrating as an eagle's. He was never known to give a false alarm. We were bear hunting at the time, and we saw his signal and hurried to camp. He said that Indians were not far off, as a few buffalo had been raised and antelope were scampering in every direction. These signs were significant to mountain men, though, of course, the game might have been raised by friendly Indians. The stock was all corralled and everything prepared for the reception of a war-party. At sunset fifteen Indians were seen advancing, one riding in advance at full speed, firing a rifle, which meant "friends."

He came boldly into camp and we soon recognized him as "Humpy," a most remarkable Indian of about twenty-five years of age. His height was only five feet two inches, and he had a large lump on his shoulders. He was a leader of war-parties, fearless and cautious, with many "coups" to his credit. These Indians had been after a war-party of Cheyennes who had stolen some Shoshone ponies. Overtaking them on the North Platte River they recovered the ponies.

They had heard shots from our party and could not understand who could be in that country with such guns, the report being much louder than theirs. They scouted and discovered boot-tracks, which mystified them even more. Finally they discovered a trapper's moccasin track and they no longer hesitated in approaching camp. We invited them to supper and conversed until past midnight, interpreting every word to the three eastern men. They took a keen interest in the conversation, and said they had not expected such intelligence from wild Indians. We told these gentlemen that the Shoshones ranked for acumen with the most advanced Indians in America,

"Humpy" told us that Washakie's village was on a creek called Gray-bull, but would soon move to the south fork of Stinking Water, and he advised us to go there on account of the many war-parties in the country. This we concluded to do, and it was while en route that we gave the gentlemen a practical illustration of Indian warfare.

We were camped on Shell Creek, and Docket, who had been out scouting, reported having seen smoke, presumably from an Indian camp. The next day, about two o'clock in the afternoon, "Silver Tip" signaled "Indians." The stock was immediately corralled, and "Silver Tip" reported having seen a small band of Indians, some on horseback, travelling direct towards camp, though he was certain they had not discovered us as yet. The men put on all arms, which, in fact, were seldom off, and the easterners began to get a little uneasy, asking if these were hostile Indians. We answered that it was a sure thing that such a party were after scalps or horses, not being particular which.

We hid in a thicket to observe their movements, and did not have long to wait before they came in sight on a rise about three hundred yards away.

They could not see camp from that side, but they had discovered our horse tracks. They approached very carefully and looked over, but could discover nothing. We counted nine on horseback and ten on foot. The Indians now consulted for some time and then the horsemen made a detour, looking closely for tracks. After crossing the creek they saw our lodge, and at once returned to the footmen on the rise. Another consultation was held, its object most likely to estimate how many men would be there with only one lodge. "Must be a trappers' lodge."

At all events, after some time passed, the footmen divided, five going above camp and five below. The nature of this movement was well, understood by the trappers, for the Indians intended to crawl through the timber and underbrush to the lodge and find out who was there.

Should they find no one they would conceal themselves until the return of the occupants and take them by surprise; then kill, scalp, and plunder. These are Indian tactics; but this time these red men were circumvented.

Three men were sent up the creek to conceal themselves about seventy-five yards from camp, and three below. They had not long to wait. The Indians approached in a careless manner without suspicion. Above camp the trappers let the Indians get within ten feet, when they jumped out, pistols in hand. Before the Indians realized what was happening they were dead.

A moment afterwards a scattering fire was heard below camp, and two Indians were seen running towards their mounted companions on the ridge.

The trappers rushed to the corral and mounted, bidding the eastern men do likewise and see an Indian fight, as it might be their only chance. The Indians on the ridge were somewhat mystified, and remained there until we were out of the timber. At the sight of us they beat a hasty retreat, but it was too late. In order to escape they should have started as soon as they heard the shots. Their horses were indifferent ones, while ours were the very pick of the plains, and could not be excelled in any country for either endurance or speed. The two footmen mounted behind the horsemen.

When we reached the ridge the Indians were about four hundred yards away and going for " all that was out," as "Silver Tip" said. They were making for the Big Horn River, about three quarters of a mile distant.

Before they had covered half the distance we were amongst them, passing in single file. By the time the last trapper passed they were all on their way to their happy hunting-grounds. As the last Indian fell the three easterners rode up, greatly surprised at the sudden termination of the fight. They had expected to see the Indians make some resistance and then they would have taken a hand.

"But you trappers do not give a person time to do a thing except follow."

They had heard just such fights described, but could not believe it possible.

We collected all the plunder the Indians had, besides scalping them, to the amusement of the gentlemen. We asked them to lift some of the hair, but could not prevail on them to do so; although after we had the scalps stretched on hoops and dried, they took half a dozen to show to their friends in the east.

That night they asked why the Indians had not used the bows and arrows which they carried in their hands. We answered that the Indians had their minds set on getting to the timber, and they did not know the quality of the men who were after them. We rode passing them on their right, because they could not use their bows and arrows on that side without turning around.

They did not know which side we would come up on, for we did not fire a shot until within ten feet, then passing in single file we delivered shots as we passed. They had no time to turn, as we passed like a whirlwind. When the last man passed the Indians were most of them dead.

Had we passed them on the left side some of us might have been hurt, though that is very doubtful, as men and horses alike were quick and active. And another thing, the closer you are to an Indian the less danger there is of getting hurt. You confuse him and he does not seem able to collect his thoughts.

These Indians were strange to us, but when shown the scalps Washakie told us that they were Pend Oreilles.

We spent a very pleasant time at the Shoshone village, especially the first evening, when we recounted to Washakie how we had trapped the Indians. He was highly pleased and said "Old trappers are wolves," meaning in Indian way of speech, hard to take in or always on the alert. He thought the Pend Oreilles were fools to think that there were no trappers at the lodge.

We gave the rest of the scalps to the Shoshones, and the young folks had a merry scalp dance, which kept up until past midnight.

We went on buffalo hunts, on bear hunts, and, in fact, gave our employers an opportunity to try their hand on every variety of game to be found in that section, much to their satisfaction.

When we reached Green River and bade our three gentlemen adieu, we were all well satisfied with the trip.

CHAPTER XXI

We moved to Henry's Fork of Green River, intending to complete preparations for our California trip at this place. Many mountain men had already congregated there.

A fearful storm set in and lasted three weeks. Our whole time was taken up in looking after stock, so as to keep them up in flesh. We cut the bark of young cottonwoods, which is very nutritious and will keep stock in good shape for a short time. We also kept a close guard both night and day, for we knew that war-parties were about. Fortune favored us, as we were not visited by any horse-stealing parties while we remained in this camp. Parties on Black and Ham Forks of Green River did not come off so well, but lost several ponies through negligence and were constantly bothered by the Indians.

Several of the men at this rendezvous had relations in Oregon and decided to go that way, visit them, and pass on to California. Others decided to take the southern route, passing through Utah. Our party selected the middle route, via Humboldt River and through the Carson Valley.

Some of the men had heard of our difficulty with the Pah Utes at Rocky Point, and thought that we might come in contact with our former antagonists. "Yes," I said; "but they have not forgotten the reception we gave them, and may conclude to give us a wide berth." We thought that nine trappers were sufficient for those Indians. We had another motive in going by this route, namely, to see if Crawford's grave had been molested. If so, those Pah Utes would better keep a long distance from us, as in that case a few more of them would be likely to suffer.

We intended to start on the 15th of February, travel by easy stages, and collect furs. We had been told that we could find a good market in San Francisco. We did not rely altogether on being able to pick up gold on the top of the ground. Newspapers telling of fabulous finds had been brought out by the fur-buyers. The news set half of the men wild, but for all that they did not credit the report in the papers. They reasoned that if gold could be found in such quantities, the Spaniards would have overrun that country centuries ago.

Parties we came in contact with urged us to throw our traps in the creek and go with them, declaring that by the time we reached California with our furs they, simply by looking for it, would have gold enough to buy our furs, horses, and everything we had.

We went to the trading-post and bought $250 worth of trinkets to trade with Carson Indians, and on the day set, packed up, intending to strike Bear River and collect furs. We reached there without any mishap and trapped down to the mouth of Malade River, securing many furs. At Malade River we were joined by several young Mormons, who camped with us that night. They were on their way to California, excited, as many others, by the gold reports. Next morning they were off by day-light.

We made quite a catch of furs here in three days, crossed Goose Creek range, trapped that stream, Raft River, and other creeks, and did remarkably well. Having as yet come across no Indians, we proceeded to the head of Humboldt River. A few Indians showed themselves, but kept clear of us. We continued down to Rocky Point and camped on our old ground. We examined Crawford's grave and found it had not been disturbed.

The Indians hovered around us, but did not approach. It was manifest they had not forgotten the merited chastisement we had administered or they would have paid us a visit. We did not set any traps, but pulled out early the next morning and made some thirty miles. Here we camped and set our traps and made a good catch. As soon as the hides were off we packed up, and made twenty miles over the same old route. We saw a few Indians at a distance, but whether they were following us or belonged to some other village, we did not know. At all events, we did not give them an opportunity to raid us or our stock. We took extraordinary precautions, catching only a few furs close to camp. The next morning we were off early and reached Humboldt Lake, but caught no beaver. The next day we reached the lower end of the lake and spent two days stretching and drying furs. Here some more Mormons arrived and camped with us over night.

Here is the starting point of the two routes across the Great American Desert, one leading to Truckee and another to Carson. We advised the Mormons to take the latter, which they did the next morning.

The next day we crossed, getting to Carson River early, and found our friends the Mormons in a sorry plight. It had been exceedingly warm the day they crossed the desert. As a result of their having urged their horses beyond endurance, they had to lay up for a week to recruit their stock. Hundreds suffered the same way when crossing this desert by not exercising proper judgment. We traded with our former friendly Indians, who were really glad to see us. They had considerable fur, all of which we got, besides collecting much ourselves.

The snow being exceedingly deep in the Sierras we camped at the base. Here some of the Mormons returned, saying that it was impossible to cross the mountains at this time. They had an Indian with them as guide. We engaged this same Indian and another volunteered to go also. As I stated before, we had treated those Indians with the greatest kindness and they were ready to do anything for us, so we accepted this last Indian's offer.

These Indians guided us through the night as easily as by daylight, for they had crossed the mountains many times. We started at nine o'clock in the evening, with forty-five head of stock, the Indians having two. On this route there are two high divides. The Indians thought we could cross the first by sun-up and get cottonwood bark for the horses.

We strung out our horses single file, the Indians in advance. When we first struck snow it was not very deep, and consequently there was considerable floundering. As the snow deepened travel became easier. The deeper the snow the more compact it is. At daylight we came to a creek with the snow eight feet deep. Before unpacking we tramped upon the snow to make it more solid. We cut down a lot of fir limbs, spread them upon the snow, and unpacked. The horses seemed to have human intelligence and would not leave the place we had tramped for them. Leaving two men to prepare breakfast, the remainder got large quantities of young cottonwood limbs, which the horses, being very hungry, relished greatly.

After breakfast all but one man rolled up in blankets and took a good six-hour slumber. This refreshed us greatly and we awoke as hungry as wolves. A meal fit for the gods was soon prepared, and we spent the afternoon in prospecting for a place to cross the creek. The water had made a tunnel under the snow, and it was some time before we could find a place to bridge. We cut fir limbs, laying them thick enough to cross on without stepping on the snow. The reader can imagine it would be no easy trick to extricate a horse should he fall through eight feet of snow into the creek below. We did not intend to take any chances, but piled the limbs thickly across the dangerous place.

It must have been 80° in the shade. The snow was settling rapidly, and the horses trampling around kept it comparatively solid. They were well supplied with bark, so they did not suffer for lack of food. The Indians thought we could make the west side of the main divide by daylight and would find grass. On the south side of the ridge we made some hoops and stretched rawhide over them, using them as snow-shoes. At two-thirty in the afternoon, when the snow was at its softest, Russell and "Scotty," accompanied by the Indians, donned temporary snow-shoes and took the supposed trail, going some three miles. This trail assisted us in the fore part of the night. Russell and "Scotty" said these Indians could excel them on snow-shoes, for the trappers were fagged out on their return to camp.

We packed up about nine o'clock, crossed the bridge, carefully leading each animal over, then mounted, stringing them out in single file. You could not get a horse to step one inch out of the trail. They would step into each other's foot tracks. We experienced no difficulty en route. Each mount would lead an animal, a certain number of loose ones following, they in turn being followed by a mount. One hour before daylight we crossed the divide, made good time, and reached the place designated by the Indians, and we found everything just as described. We camped on a bare spot, cooked and feasted; the horses nibbling green grass much to their delight. Grass grows under the snow in this region.

According to our reckoning this was the third day of July. As far as the snow was concerned our difficulties were over, though we still had some snow to cross. The Indians advised us to pack up at midnight, while the snow was the hardest, and we would be out of it by daylight. At eleven o'clock the next day we reached Hangtown.

Some miners—Americans and Mexicans— were located on the creek. Of the Americans all but two had come to California by the Panama route. The two mentioned were trappers who had come with Fremont. Thousands must have come by water in 1848, as these miners spoke of a town on Sacramento River called Georgetown where considerable mining was going on.

A small town was starting up here with one small store. After staying here three days we learned how to mine and save gold by a rocker and a pan. The dirt is stripped away to a depth of three or four feet, then the gold is panned out from what they call the pay dirt. This is quite different from picking up gold on top of the ground.

On the 9th of July we arrived at Sacramento, a small town then, but full of life. We put up our lodge outside of town and had many visitors; for, being dressed in fringed buckskin, a custom among free trappers, we were quite a curiosity.

Three of our men could speak Spanish, and the Mexicans gave them all the news about the mines. They claimed that the best mining section was towards the north, on the Yuba. We remained here ten days, and in the meantime disposed of our furs to a Mexican Don, who paid us our price.

After we had settled everything we bought picks, pans, rockers, crevice spoons, rubber boots, slickers, and flannel overshirts. We were transformed from trappers into miners. Packing up our mining outfit we started north, not knowing whither we were going and not caring. One thing was certain, we had set out to see some mining. None of us relished pick and shovel work, having never used these implements except to dig a few rifle-pits. However, we went cheerfully along, visiting several places where mining was in progress. We set up our lodges, taking turn about looking after the stock and cooking, the others staking off mining claims. We continued thus until the spring of 1853 with indifferent success. I saw as many men out of funds in California in those days as I have seen anywhere, in spite of the fact that work was plentiful. But the country was overrun with gamblers and round-ers, generally hard characters. Many of them died with their boots on, while many who merited the same fate escaped.

At this time we were at Little York, and some of the miners who had interests in the claims had gone to prospect some other creeks, promising to be back in a few days. They had left their clothing, and some of them con-siderable money. Their friends became uneasy at their long-continued absence, when news was brought to town that Lawyer Lewis had been hor-ribly butchered at Auburn. Lewis had his tent pitched outside the village, not far from an Indian camp. The morning following the murder the Indians dis-appeared.

Lewis was a great favorite with the miners, and when his fate became known a council was held by the miners and business men, who decided the Indians guilty.

There were very few arms among the miners. Those who had crossed the plains had rifles, but they had made crowbars of them.

CHAPTER XXII

The news brought in of miners being found stripped, scalped, and otherwise mutilated created almost a panic among the prospectors. These generally travelled either alone or with one or two companions, and seldom carried arms to defend themselves with.

A general rumor was afloat that the Indians from the Colorado River west, and from the Mexican line to the British-American border, had united against all the white men.

News came that Governor Joe Lane of Oregon was fighting Indians on Rogue River and that the Indians in the Walla Walla country had declared war. Everything looked gloomy and desperate to the many miners, and daily councils were held, especially by the business men.

Our outfit was almost everywhere known among the miners as the "Mountaineer Miners." We had retained all our arms and horses and had each two suits of buckskins, one as a Sunday suit, so Noble said.

Six of us had traded our Hawkins rifles for Sharps rifles, brought in by emigrants. The barrels of the Hawkins rifles made good substitutes for crowbars. These were the first Sharps rifles we had seen and we found them most effective weapons, our only criticism being that the triggers pulled too hard. We had a gunsmith resight them and fix the triggers, and securing a lot of tape caps and ammunition, we practised for several days. They were equal in accuracy to our old rifles and far superior in effectiveness.

A dispatch was received from the business men of Nevada City asking us to come there at once and attend a council relative to the Indian problem. We dressed in our buckskins and mounted our war-horses, as Docket insisted on calling them. "Scotty" was left to take care of camp. At three in the afternoon we reached Nevada City and found the place full of miners. A person looking on as we rode down the street would have imagined a circus in town. Every man, woman, and child in the town rushed out of the houses, and many of them looked as if they thought we had come to capture the city.

We rode to the California Hotel, where we were met by the leading business men and city officials. Here we dismounted and our horses were put in the stable, with orders to take the best of care of them. We were then escorted to the reception room, where a tempting repast awaited us.

After feasting to our hearts' content we advised the citizens to hold council at once. Mr. A. L. Graham, a banker, presided, and he said that the object of the council was to consider the ways and means of putting a stop to the slaughtering of prospectors and miners by the Indians. He read a paper recounting the number of miners who had been found scalped and otherwise mutilated, and dwelt upon the barbarous manner in which Lawyer Lewis had been treated. When through with the paper, he called the attention of the assemblage to our party, remarking that these mountaineers were the ones to take a leading part in deciding what to do in the disposition of the Indians. All were satisfied that these murders had been committed by the Indians.

We were called upon to address the meeting. As Perkins was the oldest we selected him to do the talking. In a few terse remarks he informed the meeting that he thought there should be no time wasted in following these Auburn Indians, as this tribe had done most of the killing. To his question as to how many lodges there were in the Auburn village, he was answered sixty. Perkins thought this signified from one hundred and twenty to one hundred and forty warriors. He also thought that fifty men armed with rifles would be sufficient to punish the Indians.

A runner was dispatched to Grass Valley, three miles distant, and one to Auburn, calling for fifty volunteers who had rifles to meet at Grass Valley that evening. There were but twelve men in Nevada City who owned rifles, although several had pistols. Horses were plenty, but there was a scarcity of saddles, blankets being used as a substitute.

We deposited most of our funds with Wells Fargo Company's bank. Up to this time we had always packed our funds, having little confidence in banks. Supper was furnished at the city's expense, and we were not allowed to pay for anything. Immediately after supper we mounted and proceeded to Grass Valley, where fifteen men had already assembled. By eight o'clock we mustered sixty-three mounted and fairly well-armed men..

Perkins was elected captain and, by order of that dare-devil Russell, I was elected first lieutenant, Evans second lieutenant, and Russell first sergeant, to his great disgust, as he said that all he knew was "how to shoot." Four pack-horses were loaded with supplies, as it was uncertain how long we would be absent, and game was not over plenty. Many of the mountains in California are grassy, with open timber, and clear of underbrush.

The best information to be had was that the Indians had gone towards the mountains, passing a small mining camp called Cold Spring. We made for this place and soon struck the Indian trail. We followed the trail, crossing a creek called Blue Canon. Here the Indians had killed three miners and burnt their cabins. The miners, who were horribly cut up, were known to several in our party. We gave them decent burial. The Indians had camped one night at this place.

We now followed the trail at a gallop wherever the ground permitted. The Indians had remained together, as we kept a sharp lookout to ascertain if they divided their village. About noon we came to a lake, and the signs showed that they had camped there that morning, as the ashes in the fires were still hot. We were certain that up to this time they had no idea that we were following. We remained at the lake one hour for lunch and then took up the trail, which led up a long ridge towards a high mountain. From the ridge the Indians must have discovered us, for we now saw signs that they had been hurrying forward.

We soon overtook their rear lookouts, who made for their outfit. The village had just reached a creek when we came in sight of it. The Indians soon had their packs off and formed a breastwork. Perkins remarked, "There is a chief who understands how to prepare for a fight." We had not looked for this from these Indians. They were armed with a few good rifles, obtained, no doubt, from miners, and had many Mexican rifles and bows and arrows.

We now divided our forces. Perkins ordered me to take twenty-five men and cross the creek, so as to make a flank movement. This was done with considerable difficulty, as the banks of the creek were very steep. When we got opposite the Indians we tied our horses behind trees for protection. Meantime the Indians were sending forth yells of defiance and firing a few shots from long range. They had no protection from our side, as the creek bank was fully six feet higher than it was on the Indian side.

Perkins had deployed his men and opened the engagement, and was gradually drawing nearer the Indians, until he was within one hundred yards of their breastwork.

About forty Indians were facing us. The women were rolling up lodges so as to make temporary breastworks against our shots. We kept creeping closer and closer, taking cover behind trees, until we got within fifty yards of the creek.

The chief was brave, and if all his warriors had been likewise, Perkins would have had a hand-to-hand combat, as the chief with eighty warriors charged him. They had covered half the distance to Perkins when the chief fell. This disheartened the others and they beat a hasty retreat to the breastworks. Here the Sharps rifles proved their superiority over the muzzle-loaders, and the rapidity of their fire astonished the Indians.

From our side we had the Indians at a great disadvantage. The edge of the bank was fringed with trees, and we were able to keep creeping nearer and nearer. The women and children soon became panic-stricken and before long the warriors also, and it was now that they suffered the most; the warriors running about within their enclosure and getting mixed up with the women and children. Almost every shot we fired took effect.

Perkins was now almost at the breastwork and we had reached the very edge of the bank. One miner in my command had an arm broken by a shot and another was shot in the ribs. "Silver Tip" had his ear split by an arrow.

The Indians now became frantic and they jumped into the creek en masse, women, men, and children all mixed up. Perkins's force charged over the breastwork and, amid the greatest screaming, howling, and yelling one ever heard, killed what few Indians were there.

About thirty of the men escaped. We captured the women and children who remained. Many of the latter had fallen, which could not be avoided, for they were mingled with the men, and the miners shot at anything that looked like an Indian.

Perkins had six wounded in his command, two quite seriously, but by careful nursing they all recovered. Russell had a close call, getting a bullet through his hat.

We captured seventy-four horses; many in the bunch had been stolen from miners. We also found seventeen white men's scalps which we took with us to show, so as to teach a lesson to those sceptics who believed in the innocence of the Indians. Besides the horses we found saddles, blankets, clothing, and about five hundred dollars in gold dust in buckskin purses.

We destroyed everything in the shape of lodges and scalped all the men. Every miner had one scalp and some two, besides a quantity of bows and arrows and guns. After the fight a council was held and many of the miners were in favor of wiping out the women and children whom we had captured, but the trappers persuaded them not to do so. We considered for some time taking the women prisoners, but concluded they would be a burden. The men who had escaped would return soon after our departure, and there was no danger that they would starve, as berries and roots were plentiful.

We constructed three travois for the worst wounded and returned to the lake at the foot of the ridge, reaching it about midnight.

At daylight six miners were dispatched to settlements to have doctors and wagons meet us at Blue Canon. We travelled slowly on account of the wounded, and reached the Canon on the second day. Fully one hundred men were there to meet us, and they were wild with elation over our victory. The miners made it appear that we trappers were more than heroes, and "Silver Tip" said it made us blush to hear such flattery. The doctors took charge of the wounded, putting them in spring wagons. We arrived at Cold Spring Hotel by sundown, and the people there would not let us cook, but made us dine at the hotel.

Next morning we prepared to start for our camp at Little York, but the citizens all protested. We must go to Nevada City and let the people see a true American mountaineer. I suppose we did look strange to them with our two big Colt revolvers, rifle, and a two-pound tooth-pick, besides our fringed buckskin suits and moccasins. When we arrived in Nevada City the whole population turned out to greet us. They were no longer depressed in spirits over all the murders, as they were satisfied the mysteries were solved and the guilty detected and punished. Even the mayor got beyond himself in a public speech, giving the trappers credit for being the "avengers of all this slaying of prospectors." He held up to view the seventeen white men's scalps, and one man in the crowd rose and pointed to a certain one, saying, "That is Lawyer Lewis's scalp."

The miners who were with us overdid the killing, saying we had wiped out over two hundred men and women. We heard afterwards that some of the ministers gave us credit for being savages and fit only to dwell among such.

Next day we brought in the seventy-four horses, twenty of which had belonged to prospectors. They were turned over to the city authorities and sold at auction, bringing in about fifty dollars per head. This money, at our request, was given to the wounded men.

The citizens offered to raise a purse for us but the offer was rejected, as we stood in no need of money. They prevailed upon us to spend the day with them, and when the stage arrived in the evening the papers were full of accounts of massacre. One large pack-train had been taken and all the packers killed except one Mexican, who had escaped and brought the news. This took place at Biglow's Lake, at the head of Truckee River. Volunteers were called for to chastise the Indians who had committed the crime.

CHAPTER XXIII

The next day we returned to Little York, where the news of our victory over the Auburns had spread like wildfire. A letter came to the mayor requesting us to go to Hangtown (now Placerville), where volunteers would be enrolled, and we went as requested. Great excitement prevailed there, and sixty men were mustered under the command of Bob Williams. We came in contact with the Indians at Biglow's Lake, where there is a prairie of some extent. The Indians were armed with lances, bows and arrows, and some Spanish flintlock guns. When we deployed on the prairie, Indians to the number of one hundred and fifty charged us. We passed through them, wheeled, and recharged, attacking the Indians in the flank. At this they became bewildered, for they had not expected to be charged in turn.

There happened to be twenty-five men in the company who had served as cavalrymen in the Mexican War. But for that fact we would have met with disastrous defeat. The volunteers' horses became unmanageable in the yelling and firing that ensued. Through it all the trappers, who had right flank in charge, remained together, striking the Indians on their left, where the Indians were three to one. Led by two chiefs and armed in part with lances they charged us, but the chiefs went down when within fifty yards of us. The Indians, seeing their chiefs fall, halted for a moment, which was fatal to them. The trappers passed through them with their Colt revolvers playing before they had recovered their presence of mind. It was a slaughter. The trappers wheeled and charged the main body of Indians and struck them on the left flank, doubling them up.

At this instant the Mexican War veterans had wheeled and charged with a yell. They were brave men, and if their horses had been trained as ours were they would have done three times the execution they did. As it was, the charge they made saved the day to us. There was one tall Indian decorated with all the barbaric splendor of war-bonnet and feathers on a fine horse, who was endeavoring to rally the Indians. The trappers saw at a glance that this chief must be gotten rid of if we were to gain the victory, and we made for the cluster of Indians he was rallying, scattered them, and killed the chief and several lesser ones. When you put a quietus on a chief you have a battle won. The Indians beat a hasty retreat up the valley, where their village was located. Russell's horse went down in this charge, but he secured the Indian's horse and soon overtook us.

In rounding a bend we came upon the pack train of mules. About sixty-five Indians who had passed through the village were at their heels. The old men and women who had witnessed the battle and its results had abandoned the village and taken to the mountains.

We burned the village and everything it contained, collected the mules and ponies, and returned to the battlefield. Only forty of us followed the Indians to their village, and in this running fight the superiority of our Sharps rifles became again apparent. When we began fighting we had forty rounds of ammunition, and we came out with from three to seven. Captain Williams gave them the credit for gaining the victory, but there is no doubt in my mind that it was due to the Colt revolvers.

The captain remarked that he had seen lots of cavalry service, but had never seen such well-trained horses as ours. I rode my Kentucky horse "Otto," and came near losing him, for a bullet passed through his ear. Perkins's horse died from wounds. "Scotty's" horse fell at the first charge, but he quickly found another mount. "Scotty" was a hero in a fight, quick as a flash, cool and collected under the most trying circumstances.

Six of the Mexican veterans and two miners fell in the fight. Many of these volunteers were poor horsemen and had never fired a pistol before. They were brave enough, but they could not control their horses. For such an engagement as we had just had, constant drill in the use of arms and in horseback riding was required.

We had buried the eight men who had fallen when thirty men arrived as a reinforcement. It was amusing to see these new arrivals scalping the Indians. The trappers showed them how to accomplish it and they were apt scholars.

Some of the trappers had received slight wounds. The only thing that annoyed them was getting blood on their buckskin suits. Buckskin is hard to clean.

A council was held to consider whether to follow up the Indians or not. Finally the captain concluded that this chastisement would prevent them from molesting any more whites.

We started on our return trip and reached Hangtown without further trouble. The owner of the mules, who lived in Marysville, was notified to come and get his property.

News had arrived that the Indians in Shasta and Trinity counties were hostile, and while we were absent had committed what is known as the Trinity massacre, slaughtering right and left, men, women, and children. Volunteers had been called for, and the captain, with his old soldiers as well as we trappers, joined the forces. When we reached Shasta City we found every one scared nearly to death, and there were many families there.

Those Indians are known as "Tar-heads," and they received a just chastisement when, in less than thirty days, more than half of them were placed hors-de-combat, which put a quietus on any further devilment on their part. The Indian Commissioners gathered the remnant of them and they became wards of Uncle Sam.

We remained in this section until 1855, when we took part in the windup of the Rogue River war. The volunteers were commanded by General Lamrick, who received his appointment through political influence. He understood nothing about military tactics and less about Indian fighting.

In 1856 the Modoc war broke out. Three companies were called out, and we belonged to what was known as the "Buckskin Rangers." Our commander was General Crosby, a third-rate lawyer, who also received his appointment by a political pull. He was a counterpart of Lamrick in knowledge of Indian fighting. Neither of them ever went into an engagement.

At the close of the Modoc war the Pitt River Indians committed the Pitt River massacre and the three companies went after them. After annihilating about half, the remainder surrendered and were placed on a reservation. The volunteers were disbanded, but we trappers remained together, mining a little until 1858.

In the spring of that year Perkins, Noble, Docket, Evans, and "Scotty" concluded to go to New Mexico. Russell remained with me. We all promised to meet again, but never did, although we often corresponded.

About this time there was great excitement over the discovery of gold on Fraser River in British Columbia, and for a while it looked as if the stampede would deplete California of her mining population. Pack-trains were rushing to Dallas, Oregon, to pack supplies to the miners on the river. Don Alvares, a Chilean, engaged Russell and myself to guide him and his two pack-trains from Yreka to Dallas. We took the east side of the Cascade range, as grass was reported scarce on the west side. This route took us through the Modoc country by Klamath lakes, but we experienced no difficulty and it was evident that the Indians had cooled down, for a while at least.

When we arrived at Dallas we met some officers from Walla Walla, who told us the commander wished to employ some experienced scouts. We were offered good pay to accompany a pack-train to Fraser River, but declined, preferring to visit Fort Walla Walla.

When we reached the Fort we saw a number of Nez Perces Indians on the parade ground surrounded by officers. We attracted considerable attention owing to our fringed buckskin and moccasins. The Indians immediately asked us in sign-language where we had come from? We answered in signs, much to the astonishment of both officers and Indians, who did not expect such proficiency from us. Colonel Wright, the commanding officer, invited us to his office and asked us many questions, which we answered truthfully, after which he engaged us as scouts.

Some little time before we reached the Fort the Yakimas, Spokane, Colville, and other tribes had declared war. Colonel Steptoe met the Palonse and Spokane tribes and was defeated. Lieutenant Caston, a nephew of General Scott, lost his life in this battle. The Nez Perces came between the hostiles and troops and saved the latter from being slaughtered.

Colonel Wright had succeeded Colonel Steptoe by order of General Harney, who in turn had succeeded General Wool as commander of the Pacific Coast. There had been a lull in Indian affairs, and Colonel Wright was anxious to find out if possible what the Indians were doing and how many warriors they could muster. This was a difficult problem for us to solve, as we were strangers in the country.

CHAPTER XXIV

Russell bought a fine unbroken horse and saddled and mounted him outside of the parade grounds, where there were rock-piles. He was an expert and fearless rider, but the moment he was in the saddle the horse began pitching furiously. The officers asked me if he would be able to "stick," and I answered "Yes, if nothing breaks."

I had no sooner spoken when the cinch broke and Russell landed on his head on one of the rock-piles. We rushed to him and found him unconscious. The doctor was immediately called and ordered to have him conveyed to the hospital. His skull was badly fractured and he never regained consciousness. On the second day he died, and I lost one of my closest friends. He was one of the bravest men I had ever known, kind and generous to a fault and a man of infinite resource. He had been in more desperate engagements than fell to the lot of many who followed prairie life for a calling. I was left alone.

I had lost my horse Otto, which had received a poisoned arrow in one of the engagements on Pitt River. Another one of my trained horses was crippled by stepping in a badger hole while in pursuit of Indians. I had purchased a thoroughbred in Yreka, calling him Hickory.

This horse I retained for many years, and he was well broken. He would lie down on a blanket and he seemed to have human intelligence. The officers wanted to buy him, but I told them he was not for sale. He would come at a gallop when I whistled, expecting sugar and some petting. The ladies said, "Hamilton, you love your horse and we don't wonder at your not parting with him."

Soon after Russell's death I was introduced to a Scotch half-breed named McKay, who was well acquainted with the country and could speak two or three Indian languages. The officers told me he was brave and could be trusted.

We held a consultation about the best way of penetrating into Indian villages. McKay had found out that the Indians were in need of ammunition and tobacco, so I proposed to the officers that we take two pack-horses loaded with the articles named, and make the Indians believe we were their friends. We would also tell them that if the officers found out that we traded ammunition they would hang us.

The council of officers approved this plan, and we began at once to prepare for the expedition.

I concluded to leave my horse "Hickory" and take Russell's horse, which was a good one. We secured two gentle ponies to pack the ammunition and tobacco, and left the Fort after dark. We made about forty miles before daylight and hunted up a spring which McKay knew of. We remained here until sundown, and that night reached the Columbia River about ten miles below the mouth of Umatilla River.

On the opposite side was a Klick-a-tat village which had joined the hostile tribes. It was about one o'clock in the morning when McKay called to them. They asked, "What's wanted?" and we answered friends, and to come over with canoes, as we wanted to cross. They came over with two and we crossed, swimming our horses.

On reaching the village we found the whole tribe assembled to see who could possibly come at that time of night. They were acquainted with McKay, but they sized me up. I was dressed in a Hudson Bay shacto coat, with a Scotch cap. These Indians were friendly with Hudson Bay employees. They feasted us with dried salmon and we told the chief what we had. After this we slept till daylight, when a council was held. The chief informed us that the Palouse and other tribes would assemble on McNatchee River that day, as the Yakimas with their great chief Kan-a-yak-a wanted to see how many warriors each tribe could furnish. He further said that they would be glad to see us with ammunition and tobacco. We traded a little with these Indians, and as a blind had to take in exchange two good ponies.

We reached the rendezvous after dark, accompanied by a delegation of Klick-a-tats, and were taken direct to the chief's lodge.

Our arrival created quite a disturbance in the village and the chief eyed us closely for some time, in fact until the Klick-a-tats told him how they crossed us after midnight and traded for some ammunition. This lulled the chief's suspicion, my Hudson Bay dress assisting.

I had acquired quite a knowledge of Chinook jargon and we conversed in this language. They asked me many questions, all of which I answered, telling them that Hudson Bay men were their friends, and that I had been sent with this ammunition and tobacco to trade with them for a few ponies. It came near choking me to tell such outrageous falsehoods.

Next day about four thousand warriors assembled, and they were a gay and proud lot of Indians, who looked with disdain on both McKay and myself. We found out all that Colonel Wright required,—the approximate number of warriors, and also that the lull was caused on account of waiting for the different tribes to gather all their outside Indians and then to hold a council. They decided to assemble all their warriors on the Spokane River and draw the soldiers on, when they would kill all the cavalry and take "walk-a-heap" (infantry) prisoners and make slaves of them.

We traded all our ammunition and tobacco, and such a trade was never made before or since. We gave all our stuff to the chief and told him to give us what ponies he thought proper. He called up the Indians who had no ammunition and issued some to each, for which we received a few ponies and not very good ones either.

That afternoon at five we started as if going west, but when out of sight of the Indians we turned south, so as to strike the Columbia opposite Wallula, at the mouth of Walla Walla River. We rode the best ponies, leading our horses. The poor ponies we left on the prairie, having no use for them. When the ponies gave out we rested for half an hour and then saddled our horses, which were, comparatively speaking, fresh. We made excellent time and at sun-up were opposite Wallula.

McKay knew where the Indians always kept canoes "cached," but we rested an hour before attempting to cross. The river is wide at this place and it takes a good horse to swim it.

We crossed without mishap and let the horses feed for two hours, after which we proceeded towards the Fort, where we arrived at ten o'clock that night. It was thirty miles from Wallula to the Fort. We reported our arrival to the officer on guard and he sent an orderly to Colonel Wright. This orderly soon returned with orders to report immediately at headquarters.

A council was in progress and we made our report. Colonel Wright was well pleased at the news that the Indians were collecting on Spokane River, and he said the campaign would be a short one. His predictions proved true. The Indians, in force estimated at five thousand strong and fairly well armed, were met by Colonel Wright with one thousand soldiers, forty Nez Perces Indians, and two howitzers, which, when the shells burst among them, doing considerable execution, frightened the Indians very badly. They beat a hasty retreat to St. Joe Mission, and the chiefs pleaded with the fathers to intercede for them. Nine chiefs were taken prisoners and held as hostages for the Indians' good behavior. We then returned to the Fort, having been absent but six weeks.

An Indian rumor had it that all tribes east of the Rocky Mountains were forming a combine against whites. The United States was getting tired of these continual outbreaks of the Indians, so I volunteered to find out whether there was any truth in the Indian rumor. I took McKay with me, also a trading outfit. We passed through recent hostile tribes, going by St. Joe Mission, and found the Indians surly, but on their good behavior.

We camped one night where Missoula, Montana, now stands, and I noticed many Indian trails converging. It struck me as an ideal spot for a trading-post, and I told McKay that if we got back from this trip with our lives I would return and establish a trading-post there, which I did late that fall.

We made the trip and found the Indian rumor false. Returning, we reported the news to Colonel Wright. I received great credit for that trip. Settling with the Government, I purchased some goods and started back to Montana, establishing a trading-post at the aforesaid place. I remained there until 1864, when I sold out and moved to Fort Benton, and opened up a business at that place. I was elected Sheriff and appointed Deputy United States Marshal. In 1869 I sold out at Fort Benton and moved to the Yellowstone Valley, intending to open a trading-post.

About this time the Sioux, Arapahoes, and Cheyennes became very hostile, even making raids on the farmers in the Gallatin Valley.

In 1874 an expedition was organized, consisting of one hundred and forty-eight men. We started in midwinter, going down the Yellowstone River, crossing at lower Porcupine Creek. We then travelled over a broken country to East Rosebud, having two small engagements en route.

On East Rosebud we had two rifle-pit engagements, repulsing the Indians in every instance with heavy loss. We then went to the Little Big Horn and had two more fights, one on Grass Lodge, where fifteen hundred Indians charged us, but we repulsed them with heavy loss. The people in Bozeman having had no tidings, concluded we were all lost.

This was the expedition which brought on the war of 1876, that was so disastrous to General Custer and his command. In that year I joined General Crook on Goose Creek, engaging as scout along with nine others.

The General took his troops to Wolf Mountains and had a fight with the Sioux and Cheyennes, losing thirteen soldiers besides having several wounded. We beat a retreat back to Goose Creek and remained there until joined by General Merritt with reinforcements. Meanwhile General Custer had been annihilated while we rested with eighteen hundred soldiers. When General Merritt joined us we moved down Rosebud to Tongue River without meeting any hostile Indians, and then to Powder River. General Terry arrived on a steamboat.

A council was held which lasted several days. In the meantime the Indians had divided, Sitting Bull crossing the Yellowstone and Crazy Horse going east until he crossed the Little Missouri, then southeast to Slim Buttes.

Our command followed Crazy Horse. We struck a Sioux village, with American Horse as chief. We captured the village and took American Horse prisoner. The chief had received a wound in the fight, from which he died that night.

The troops had been living on horse-meat and were anxiously looking for supplies. The command proceeded to White Wood Creek, where supplies arrived from Deadwood. The troops were given a week to recruit up in and then proceeded to Custer City, remaining there a few days.

From Custer City we went to Camp Robinson, capturing a few Indians on the road.

At Fort Laramie I resigned and returned to the Yellowstone Valley, locating at Columbus, Montana, then known as Stillwater. At eighty-two years I am hale and hearty and always spend a part of each year in the mountains trapping; thankful that I can still enjoy and appreciate the wonderful beauties of nature.

THE END